THE POWERFUL PROACTIVE PARENT'S GUIDE TO PRESENT PARENTING

EMMA GRANT

NOTEBOOK PUBLISHING

First published in 2019 by Notebook Publishing,
20–22 Wenlock Road, London, N1 7GU.
www.notebookpublishing.com

ISBN: 9780993589881

Typeset by Notebook Publishing.

To my children, Holly and Dylan, for allowing me to share their personal anecdotes and for being amazing children and teachers.

To my husband Paul, for always believing in me and for loving and supporting me in all that I do.

To my brothers Mark, Andrew, and also Ken in heaven:
We were all good children!

To every child I've ever known, loved or worked with: thank you!

CONTENTS

PRAISE FOR EMMA GRANT

I loved this book too! I found myself wanting to stop editing and go cuddle my boys, play, and teach, and parent. You are inspiring. I am sure many parents will feel the same. I can't wait to see both of these books out there and get my first copy! You have done a marvellous job. I loved too your delivery. You didn't make me feel guilty in areas I could be doing better; you inspired me and gave me tools to improve.

Your book is full of heart, common sense, and addresses the many areas we simply tend to slack on, or just don't have the proper technique or encouragement in. Parenting is a joy, but is also a job. You have laid out clearly in a usable and relatable way how to get through day after day after day, all while finding the joy again in parenting. And yes, you can quote me on that!

I consider myself privileged to have been a part of your book, even in a small way of deleting commas. Lol! I can't wait to see more from you. You have a skill for writing and a wonderful message to share.

Sending a big hug.

—*Marni Macrae*
Mum to Edain, Sarah, Joe, Toby, Noah, Dominic, and the rascal Lucas

Just finished reading, it was really insightful... I was really engrossed in it... I love the UURSELF method. I am going to start putting this into practice. I thought it was a very well thought out piece and was full of advice without sounding like this is how parenting should be done like most other parenting books!! You give an honest open description of what it is like to be a parent in a very competitive and stressful time. ... You speak with experience and that is what parents look for. ... Each chapter made me realise that all children ask for is your time and attention. We need to involve ourselves with activities a lot more and stop being so dictated by social media and gadgets! Made lots of notes from it especially about taking children to a nursery or school before they attend and for them to be able to ask any questions before hand. ... We have been very lucky with the boys as they have never shown any anxiety with new situations or people. They didn't look back on their first day in playgroup. I was so relieved as I witnessed so many children who were literally clinging to their parent. ... I felt so sad for them and could feel their frustration...

P.S. We are potty training at the moment... All valuable items are now under lock and key! I really enjoyed reading it and hope you will be writing more.

—Lucy Pryce- Griffiths, Mum to Rowan & George

Some of the points about the book is: It's easy to read, very readable for all backgrounds, great ethos and focuses on the parents as a person as well as children, it's really excellent!

—Katherine Carreira, Mum to Jorge & José

Emma is one of the most intuitive and knowledgeable childcare professionals that I have ever had the pleasure of knowing. Emma is friendly, caring and respectful. She endeavours to provide a warm, comfortable and safe environment inclusive to all children and their respective needs.

—Emma Davies, mother to Molly, Thomas and Ieuan

Harry has been going to Emma's for over two years now, I was initially concerned as it was his first experience with a childminder but Emma put my mind as ease from the moment I met her. Harry absolutely loves his time with her and the other children, to the point where he sometimes doesn't want to leave when I come to pick him up! Its abundantly clear that Emma thoroughly enjoys what she does, and this is reflected in the positive experiences Harry has with her. Thank you so much, Emma!

—*Emma Turner, Mum to Harry*

My grandchildren Jac and Bella have been looked after by Emma and Paul Grant since November 2012. They are awesome childminders and Emma in particular has been a wonderful support to me since I took over full time care of my grandchildren 7 years ago. It is such a huge comfort to me to know that the children are in safe hands and the care they receive is exemplary. Emma is always available to give advice and I am proud to consider her a very close friend. She is one special lady!

—*Elizabeth Campbell, grandmother to Jac & Bella*

My 8-month old daughter settled in with Emma and Paul really well; they have been truly caring and loving. Through each stage of development Emma adopted methods of play and learning to suit, incorporating all activities to suit her age among the other children. This has always given me great confidence as a parent and I've had no doubt that my daughter is in good hands.

Emma has also shared some great tips and suggestions on behavioural and developmental issues i.e. tantrums, potty training etc. and keeps me informed of all the highlights (first steps and words). All the photos Emma sent of days out and keeping us updated on daily activities will be forever cherished and will serve as happy memories to look back at.

Overall, Emma Grant is a smart, caring and creative child carer that I trust. Ciara loves you both and will miss you dearly!

—*Sarah, mum to Ciara*

I couldn't be happier or more content with having Oscar in Emma's care. Her support and care of Oscar and the input the she has into his development is amazing. Due to work commitments Oscar started with Emma at 9 months, and it was a huge decision to choose how he would be cared for and by whom. Emma made this so much easier, we instantly felt comfortable with Emma and her home. Oscar is nearly 2 now, and is a happy, well rounded little boy. The environment is like a part of our extended family, where he learns from interaction with adults and children of different ages. Nothing is too much trouble, with daily updates, quarterly newsletters and photos of everything they've been doing and where they've been. Emma is also able to offer support, a listening ear and advice – as first-time parents our journey has been a huge learning curve, but hearing Emma's, non-judgemental advice, due to being in childcare for so long is really reassuring.

—Kim & Neil Haworth, Mum & Dad to Oscar.

Emma cared for Lauren full time while she was an infant, this stage of development was crucial. I felt relaxed about going to work every day knowing she was being cared for in a homely, safe environment where she was happy and progressing well. As a childminder I found Emma professional, she was very aware of stages of development and understood issues such as separation anxiety, she always kept me informed and at the same time she was friendly and easy to get on with, so much so we became very close friends and Emma and Paul are our childrens Godparents!

—*Natalie and Alex Criddle, Mum & Dad to Lauren, Nathan and Ella*

Thank you, Emma, for everything you have done for William, he was a bit upset this morning knowing it was his last day with you as he always looked forward to you picking him up. This of course highlights the fact that he thinks the world of you. You have a special way about you which children are drawn to and you have given William a lovely home to home approach when you took care of him. Thanks again Emma-we'll both miss you looking after him.

—Sharon Leckey, Mum to William & Isobel

My youngest was cared for by Emma and Paul and she absolutely adored them and their children! Wonderful family and I was genuinely sad when my daughter left their care. You will have peace of mind knowing your children are in safe hands with them. Highly recommend them to anyone, looking for childcare.

—Lucy Griffiths, Mum to Amy

Thank you so much for all you have done for us and Rocco he has come on so much and thats all down to you! We will miss you all very much, wish he could stay with you forever!

—Ruth, Mum to Rocco

Emma and Paul were amazing looking after my daughter at a difficult time. Now Rosie is in full time school and doesn't need a childminder but regularly says how much she misses them. A wonderful family.

—Ruth, Mum to Rosie

Emma and Paul have been looking after my children for the last few months and what a difference I have noticed in both children they're so happy there and my eldest is always talking about Emma, Paul and their children and how she sees them as family. It's amazing how fast both children settled in they were made to feel so welcome and it made me at ease. I have had comments off other parents at the schools they do pickups from of how well looked after my children are in their care and how much you can see they care about the children! Both Paul and Emma are fantastic childminders and I couldn't ask for better!

—*Hannah Humphries, Mum to Maddie & Louie*

Emma and Paul looked after my son Leo for a short while but he will definitely remember them for life! They settled him in so well and he loved spending time with them and being around all the other children. I'm so grateful for everything they did for him and how much he learnt. If I ever need future childcare I will definitely be asking for a place for Leo. Thank you, guys xx

—*Zoe Ashton, Mum to Leo*

Emma and Paul have done an outstanding job for the past two years with looking after my two girls but not only looking after but helping raise my girls. The girls have gained friends and have had an amazing two years. We will all miss seeing Emma and Paul and wish them the best for the future.

—*Chelsea Williams, Mum to Mikhaila & Serenity*

OVERVIEW

CHAPTER 1: PROACTIVE PARENTING

Chapter 1 focuses on prevention as opposed to intervention. In essence, proactive parenting. Simply put, being proactive is taking action in advance and pre-empting our children's moves and emotions.

It sounds like a word you would find in business books—that's because it is.

I've found that we have to approach parenting sometimes like running a successful business if we want to be a success at it and produce successful children. After all, our children are our business.

CHAPTER 2: AUTO PILOT PARENTING

Understanding our own habitual ways of behaving and avoiding auto pilot parenting is what we'll address next in chapter 2 as we become more consciously aware of our own bad behaviour and how that affects our children.

CHAPTER 3: PRESENT PARENTING

Present Parenting is consciously parenting by staying present in the moment and being aware of everything going on around us. It's thinking before we respond, not just about what's going on but possibly why?

This chapter provides some simple steps on how we can learn to let go of control and learn to go with the flow, as well as simple exercises offering ways we can all become more conscious as parents and more present in the moment.

CHAPTER 4: END THE BATTLE AND WIN THE WAR

As we are one team, and since the last chapter has taught us to lighten up, now, if we want our children to do as we say, we have to let them have their own way! As we sever that umbilical cord once and for all, we'll choose our battles wisely, and as we develop the art of intervention, we'll discover how confidence conquers when we follow our own rules.

It's easy to see unwanted behaviour as the main issue and to overlook the real reasons behind that behaviour that's causing them to misbehave.

Here we'll find out why children misbehave and what motivational methods work best to modify that unwanted behaviour?

CHAPTER 5: THE 5 GOLDEN RULES

No Behaviour Coaching would be complete without rules, so chapter 5 will address the 5 Golden Rules to Making the Rules.

CHAPTER 6: HOW TO MAKE THE PERFECT CHILD

Through accentuating the positives, we'll see how unique our children are, but how their behaviour, you may or may not be surprised to find, is not so unique. We'll explore how not all of our children's imperfections are really that bad, it's just a matter of how and who is judging them? And to prove how our children's imperfect traits are actually perfect, we'll consider the following;

PERFECTLY GOOD AND BAD TRAITS

1. CONSCIENTIOUS OR INFLEXIBLE?
2. PERSISTANT OR NAG?
3. CONFIDENT OR ARROGANT?
4. ASSERTIVE OR BOSSY?
5. ENTHUSIASTIC OR HYPERACTIVE?
6. HUMOUROUS OR CLASS CLOWN?
7. OPINIONATED OR INTOLERANT?

CHAPTER 7: THE ART OF POSITIVE, EFFECTIVE BEHAVIOUR COACHING

In Chapter 7 we will unravel the mystery of miscommunication and misunderstandings and the art of coaching our childrens behaviour, by playing by the rules and using motivational methods to help us, including the secrets to motivation and negotiation skills, which is something we will need to get good at. All while learning how to stay positive when confronted with those, terrifying, toddler tantrums, in order to hug it out instead of time out.

CHAPTER 8: OUTSIDE INFLUENCES

It's time to uncover in this chapter the 'outside influences' in our children's lives that can sometimes seem out of our control such as friends, social media, You Tubers, computer games, films, celebrities, and the news.

As our children become older, it's more important than ever not to take our eyes off the ball (or off our children, so to speak).

CHAPTER 9: POWERFUL PARENTS—YOU, THE INFLUENTIAL ROLE MODEL

Before we can positively influence our children, in this chapter, we'll identify who or what has influenced us in our own lives and work to understand how that has affected us today in our parenting roles. This chapter will also highlight the importance of walking our talk. As parents, we have the great privilege, power, and ability to create happy, healthy, and successful children. In the final chapter, we'll discover what we need to be an inspiring role model.

INTRODUCTION

THE POWER IS IN OUR HANDS

WE ALL HAVE PHENOMENAL power as parents, don't you think? We have been gifted with the very powerful position of creating and raising another human being—someone with the potential to benefit society and even change the world.

Right now, you'll never know the impact your child may have upon the planet. But by the end of this book, you'll soon see how you can positively influence it!

Other people, such as friends and teachers, play an important role in our children's lives. But influencing our children is not something we want other people to take responsibility or credit for.

And it's certainly not worth leaving to chance.

FIRST LOVE

Our children believe we have all the answers to everything in the universe.

We are the first people they meet, love, and trust, and the ones who provide for their every need.

As parents, we can put the world to rights, overcome challenges, turn fear to love, and kiss it all better when things go wrong. Making us heroes in the eyes of our children.

If we can lead by example, our faithful children, like willing disciples, will follow us as our number one fans. Putting us in the perfect position to teach them whatever we wish them to learn. This is great news, as it means we are halfway there to influencing them in the direction we want them to go in.

So, why then do we feel so powerless in managing our children's behaviour?

Assuming you have already read my first book, *The Confident Parent's Guide to Raising a Happy, Healthy & Successful Child,* you'll already know that you need confidence and a routine to raise happy, healthy, and successful children.

Yet despite those two things, managing our children's unwanted behaviour is still the most difficult thing to master when it comes to parenting.

But master it we soon will!

We want a lasting approach not a quick fix solution though. And to work long term, our methods need to be consistent, fair, positive, and effective. We also need to behave appropriately ourselves, which can often be challenging when our children are pushing us to our limits and triggering our angry buttons.

RULES: THE SECRET KEY TO MANAGING BEHAVIOUR.

Rules keep our children on track when they veer off course. They ensure routines are followed, and they also help us to determine when our children are actually misbehaving or not.

Rules are the key to managing unwanted behaviour.

Routines are the key to preventing it.

The two together help us as much as our children to behave appropriately.

As long as we remain confident and consistent, and don't give in to rebellion no matter what, then eventually, our children will see that we mean business.

When they realise that 'This is the way it's going to be from now on', they will learn acceptance. Acceptance is something we will also be practicing as parents in this process too.

Once our children come to understand (and believe me, over time— they will) that what we are trying to achieve is all for their own good, they will happily adjust their behaviour.

And once we realise that what we are doing is for everyone's good, we too will adjust and learn to go with the flow more.

No one else could ever take the place of you or your child. Even a second, third, or fourth child will have their own unique place in your heart that cannot be replaced or replicated by another. However, all of us at some point get clouded by the deception that we are surrounded on the school yard, or at soft play, by seemingly perfect parents with perfect children.

We all know those parents who seem to calmly glide successfully and effortlessly through all the usual parenting challenges in a confident manner, leaving the rest of us to look on in awe and envy, clueless as to why we, with our rebellious little monsters, seem so different?

Here lies another problem and the reason we lack confidence—we keep comparing our children to other people's children and comparing ourselves to other parents. This then creates competition, which is pointless because every parent and child is unique. What works well for your sister Jenny's children won't necessarily work the same for your own. And what the other mums at the school do to manage their children's behaviour may not suit you or your child.

In reality, we may not be a deity with all the answers or be perfect parents, but all it takes is a little understanding, patience, love, time, and common sense to be a positive, influential role model for our children to follow.

THAT COMMON SENSE IS NOT SO COMMON!

Most of us know that we should exercise, eat at least five portions of fruit and vegetables a day, and get a good night's sleep. It's common sense, but how many of us actually do that every day?

And if we don't behave as we should, how can we expect our children too?

Just knowing what to do doesn't make it automatically happen.

As Voltaire's dictum goes; "That common sense is not so common."

We know what we should be doing to help our children, but often, we just don't know how or where to start.

I'm a parent just like you. As parents, we are all busy, stressed, and short of time. Leaving most of us confused about what we should be doing, when, and why.

Over the last sixteen years as a Registered Childminder, Parenting Coach, and Hypnotherapist working in partnerships with countless children and their parents, I understand the daily struggles that all parents and children face. And from that privileged position, I'm lucky to be able to understand situations from both an adult and child's perspective. And being able to understand both sides is the secret to all happy, fulfilling relationships and managing our children's behaviour appropriately.

There are many experts out there these days telling us what we should or shouldn't be doing, but their advice is constantly changing. One year, co-sleeping with our baby is best, the next, it can be dangerous. Then we are advised not to wean a baby until they are at least six months old—until the next year when it changes to four months! One popular method of behaviour modification highlighted in the media championed the naughty step, until it was discovered to be humiliating, ineffective, and damaging to children's well-being.

Couple that with well-meaning friends and family offering their 'constructive contribution' and advice (or criticism depending on who's giving it), and parenting is a mystery to most of us. It would seem that we are damned if we do and damned if we don't. Leaving most of us confused and lacking in confidence regarding our parenting capabilities.

Whether we are an experienced parent with a tribe of little people, or a new, soon to be first-timer, what we all need is some sensible solutions, reassurance, comfort, and confidence to guide us through the parenting journey.

That way, we can enjoy the parenting process and provide our children with solutions, reassurance, and the comfort and confidence they need to be happy, healthy, and successful.

This Book won't guarantee you will unravel the mystery of parenting success overnight, but hopefully, it will guide you in the right direction, making you feel more empowered as a parent so you can look forward to spending time with your child as opposed to dreading outings or social occasions.

WHAT HAPPENED?

Surely, none of us would have chosen to become parents in the first place had we thought we would end up angry, frustrated, nagging, stressed out, sleep deprived, nervous wrecks.

We become parents with the sole intention of enjoying every moment with our children, and to love, cherish, and appreciate the joy they bring.

Okay, admittedly, before our bundles of joy arrived, we envisioned a beautifully decorated nursery where our new arrival would sleep like a baby peacefully through the night.

We never thought as far as the colic, teething, bedwetting, sleepless nights, and the crayon all over the walls, or the bombsite a toddler would create in their once beautiful bedroom. And it's doubtful any of us could have imagined tantrums in the supermarket and brawls on the playground as we daydreamed of building sandcastles at the beach and sunny days playing in the park.

But have our children let us down, or have we all just been naively seduced by the notion of what parenting should be like?

Resolving conflict and upset can be difficult if we believe our children and their behaviour are to blame for how we are feeling. Or if we think that they are the reason why we react the way that we do toward them.

What if, as parents, we have just developed a bad habit of reacting to our children? And our children have just developed a bad habit of responding to us?

What if the actual problem all boils down to not having enough time to spend, misunderstanding our children's behaviour, and not being consciously aware of our own behaviours that are affecting our children—not our children's behaviour itself.

The truth is, parenting can be a joyous experience full of fun times together. But like any other relationship, it does take a lot of time and patience to build rewarding, loving relationships with our children.

Whatever parenting tools or techniques we use, from naughty steps to never saying 'No' to our children, and no matter how much advice we receive from others, without enough time to devote to our children, it's all worthless and ineffective.

The good news, however, is that it only takes time to build those happy, healthy, and successful relationships with our children.

But we have to make the time for it.

TIME: BOTH THE PROBLEM AND SOLUTION

Having too many things on our 'To do List' takes our time and attention away from our children. We would certainly all be more effective and more relaxed parents if we didn't have so many plates spinning in the air. The frustration arises when we try to keep all those plates in the air and the inevitable happens—we drop a few.

As our children are those closest to us, they're naturally more loving and forgiving than anyone or anything else in our lives. We can certainly put them off a lot easier than we can our Boss or our Tax Return. Sadly, for those reasons, they are the ones who suffer the most when we are busy doing too many other things.

But not enough time is not the real issue. It's how we spend the time we do have with our children that counts. Even when we are spending time with our children, we tend to still be thinking of past work or relationship issues or fretting about the future instead of concentrating on enjoying time with them.

Understandably, with our busy schedules and hectic lifestyles, our minds can and do easily wander from the trivia of our children's conversations or complaints, to our more pressing grownup issues.

If, like most of us, while juggling everything, you're finding parenting overwhelmingly stressful at times, fear not, there is an easier way. I promise.

I've been where you are, sleep deprived, stressed, and lacking confidence in my parenting abilities. I found a way through it, and you will too!

But it means taking action to pre-empt and prevent situations arising before they actually occur instead of reacting to them once it's too late. When we are not being proactive in our approach to parenting, that's when all the tears, tantrums, and struggles happen. Making us feel powerless, as if our children and their behaviour is out of our control.

This book will help you regain some of that control, without being a controlling parent. There is a big difference.

There's an easier way that like a magical formula, once habituated, creates happy, healthy, and successful children and parents.

I know because I've used it with great success with my own children, and I've shared it with countless parents and children alike too.

It's a stress-less path once you're on it, but getting on it can be a challenge to begin. But not beginning and staying hopelessly stuck and stressed is the only other option.

The intention of this book is to mainly help you become more mindfully present and conscious as a parent and to enjoy the parenting journey as much as your child enjoys being your child, making you consciously aware throughout all the good times, while offering solutions to coaching positive behaviour. As a result, you may or may not be surprised to find that you positively change as much as your child.

You may find some parts of the book or certain messages repetitive. That's done on purpose because they are important points, and repetition is the key to solidifying learning and lasting change. It can take our minds several times of hearing, reading, or seeing something to take it in and accept it. So please, enjoy this effortless learning as you read.

I recommend you also grab a notebook (or ideally a journal that you can continue to use after reading this book) and pen as you read, as there will be plenty of opportunities for you to take part throughout in some simple self- reflective exercises. These aren't compulsory, but you'll gain the most benefit from this book if you do them. Writing things down excels the reflective learning process, and being proactive means taking some action, so let's turn the page to discover how!

CHAPTER 1:
PROACTIVE PARENTING

WHAT EXACTLY IS PROACTIVE Parenting?

It sounds like a word you would find in business books—that's because it is. I've found that we have to approach parenting sometimes like running a successful business if we want to be a success at it and produce successful children. After all, our children are our business. We can't leave it to chance or allow anyone else to take credit or responsibility for how they turn out. As parents, we have the most power and control to influence them and if we do so positively, we will end up with a happy, healthy, and successful child.

Yet most of us feel we are constantly reacting to situations and our children's behaviour in the heat of the moment. Now, I'm an advocate of what I call 'Present Parenting' which is what we'll explore in more detail later on in this book. Present parenting is about living in the present moment and being conscious of the time spent with our children. But when it comes to managing our children's behaviour, we have to stop, breath, think and more than ever, be conscious of what's going on. That may mean analysing events leading up to our children's unwanted behaviour to see what triggered them. If we overreact and jump in too soon to discipline or get angry, we can't solve anything. We need to be calm and conscious.

Usually, parents react unconsciously out of habit to unwanted behaviour and situations, usually fuelled with emotions. As proactive parents, we want to prevent those circumstances from arising in the first place.

I know it's hard not to get upset and angry with our children sometimes, but we can lessen the chances of that happening by pre-empting problems before they affect our children and planning ahead in advance. Taking action to prevent problems as opposed to dealing with them or reacting once they have occurred. In essence, it's proactive parenting, it's hands-on parenting. And it's the simple things that can make all the difference.

Any environment we take our children into has different effects at different times of the day, so we have to learn how to pre-empt our children's moves and emotions in advance. It's thinking ahead of situations and how they may affect our children and being sensitive to their individual needs and emotions. This proactive approach enables us to take the necessary steps to make things easier, not only for our children, but ourselves too. This helps us to become more organised and in control, and as a result, increases our self-confidence, resulting in a lot less stress for everyone.

As a childminder caring for children varying in age from eleven weeks to eleven years, being proactive is a necessity. I have to be one step ahead at all times as a matter of health and safety. A simple day out to the beach can be like a military operation. But always, all the children know:

- How I expect them to behave.
- What we will do before, during, and after our visit.
- What to do if there's a problem such as someone goes missing or is lost.

Thankfully, and lucky enough, that has never happened to a child I've cared for (other than my own), which is what I credit proactive parenting for. If it did or should it do so in the future, I know I would have told all the children what to do in the event of that happening. It's not being paranoid or overly anxious, it's being proactive.

Now, you may only have one child to care for so may not feel a backup plan necessary on an outing. But there's been numerous times where I have found many lost toddlers wandering around a supermarket in tears while their parents are frantically searching for them. It happens every day.

A simple; 'If you can't find me, go straight to the security guard at the door dressed like a policeman' helps reduce this stress and prevents them crying to a random stranger or wandering out to the car park to find us where different danger could present itself.

I say this because it happened to me with my own child when they were younger. And I don't want it to happen to you if you can avoid it.

I can still feel that panic as I realised I didn't know where my child was, what they were doing, or who they were with.

As a parent, I bet you can imagine that feeling now. It's a sinking, sick feeling of impending doom and disaster as a whole host of catastrophic images flash through your mind.

Then, relief suddenly washes over you as you spot them holding hands with a lovely lady who's helping them search for you while your little one is innocently smiling, clutching onto a bag of sweets that had tempted them to wander off.

PREVENTION NOT INTERVENTION

Prevention is preferable to intervention, but we can't keep our eyes fixed on our children constantly. We can be proactive and take measures to keep them close, such as holding hands and using reins. There will, however, still be times when, like Houdini, they escape. We just have to be prepared for those times.

We can't stop our children exploring, experimenting, pushing boundaries, becoming ill, or getting cuts and bruises sometimes. What we can do is soothe, remove, or avoid the emotional distress that is often accompanied with those incidents.

We can also take measures to proactively keep them healthy by providing them with a nutritious, balanced diet, a regular routine that includes sleeping, exercise, recreation, love, and time with us, and keep them safe by childproofing their environment.

Children are into everything, everywhere. Anything within arm's reach that's attractive to their curious natures such as glass, china, ornaments, cables, cords, kitchen appliances, utensils, keys, phones, remote controls, I-pads, laptops, and curious chemicals are enticing. Whatever they can grab onto to steady themselves or break their fall, valuable or not, will succumb to those little, clumsy, unstable hands and feet. It's an accident waiting to happen. Don't invite it, be proactive and take a look around your home environment now, is it childproof ready?

If it's like any normal home, it won't be. If you already have older children, this is more so true, as their toys can present potential disaster. I'm constantly searching for tiny pieces of Lego or stray beads or coins that the older children have dropped within crawling reach of a baby. It's an ongoing quest in my house.

Ensuring these things are out of reach, minimalizing the home, and keeping certain rooms child friendly spaces that are safe to explore is essential. Taking these precautionary measures need not be forever. They can be re-evaluated over time. Simply adding stair gates to the stairs and room doors (especially the kitchen), and around the home managing cables, cords, storing chemicals, liquid soap tablets, medication, batteries, tools, valuable electronics, or ornaments out of reach makes life easier, safer, and less stressful for everyone.

Everything in sight that we try to forbid a child is a massive temptation. As soon as we say 'Don't touch this!' or we keep moving something out of their reach, we engage in their game, and they will make it their mission to get that prize. It's a game they are determined to win, and no parent can have eyes in the back of their head, watching their child twenty-four seven.

AT WHAT COSTS?

To ensure safety and damage limitation of our material possessions, we must pre-empt their moves, emotions, and reactions.

Planning for prevention is a must, if you don't you'll soon discover intervening when they are halfway through their demolition is too late.

At what costs are we willing to wait, before it's too late?

It's not only our valuable possessions or the safety aspect to consider, even when buying toys, we need to take a more proactive approach to purchasing.

It's not a good idea to give a young child an expensive toy, such as a train set, unless we expect it to get damaged. This is only setting them up to fail, and there's no point blaming them when they do what can only be expected and break it! Children don't play with toys properly like adults would. In their vivid and curious imaginations, there's no right or wrong way to play with a toy, anything goes as they experiment with gravity.

That's why not buying or allowing our children to play with anything we don't expect to get broken is best. A good trick I've found is to look at any new toy that we give a child as broken already. This is also a great money saving technique that will prevent needlessly overspending on expensive toys (remember this while Christmas and Birthday gift shopping and you'll save a fortune).

Our children don't understand our motives, but we need to. Prevention is our primary responsibility as parents. No need to get neurotic though and worry endlessly over this. Worry is a wasted energy that we could better use being proactive and taking action instead.

We've addressed the physical environment, now it's time to delve into the mental and emotional aspects of becoming a proactive parent.

Here are a few pointers to help us.

Proactive Parenting Pointers

Below are the Proactive Parenting Pointers that we need to ask ourselves and address in advance:

- What is it our children need?
- When do they need it?
- Why do they need it?
- Then provide them with what they need, before they actually need it.

That is, in essence, Proactive Parenting.

TIME TO CHECK OUT

We all have needs, but we need to know when and how to prioritise those needs. Children can't usually wait—and babies never can. Their needs must be met or at our peril. I don't mean we need to give them everything they want. Want and need are different. They may want a new toy at the supermarket, this however, is not something they need.

Therefore, we shouldn't give in and give them the object of their desire, despite their tears and tantrums showing us up in public. On the other hand, tiredness is a need, so, for example, if we want to avoid a tantrum in the middle of the supermarket, a proactive approach would mean not taking our child shopping after a busy day, especially if they are tired. Instead, we would proactively pre-empt their needs before they escalated into demands (i.e. a tantrum). Realising they were tired, rather than going shopping, we would go home and put them to bed while we do the shopping online or postpone shopping until after their nap or the next day.

Seems pretty obvious, but how often do we expect our children to fit in with our plans because we have to go somewhere or do something?

When busy or under pressure, we do this regardless of how we think they will respond.

In the busy life of parenting, this is a common dilemma that we all face daily. Unfortunately, though, when we miss or overlook our children's cues and needs, for whatever reason, this becomes the catalyst for unwanted behaviour.

We have to learn how to manage our expectations realistically and become sensitive to our children's needs.

GREAT EXPECTATIONS

When we can manage our own expectations and take a proactive approach to parenting, we can pre-empt what our children need, when, and why.

If they usually eat their lunch at twelve thirty, and it's now one pm, and at that time they hadn't eaten, we would know they needed food as they would be getting hungry. All we would have to do is provide that food before their sugar levels dropped and they were crying out for it.

We cannot always expect our children to fit in with our plans or do as we say. Proactive Parenting is being able to adapt to our children and their needs at times, especially in those all-important first few years. If we cannot fit into our children's routines or address their needs, then there will always be a conflict of interest.

A hungry baby needs a feed when they need it, a tired toddler needs a nap when they feel tired, and a teenager needs reassurance when they are feeling emotional. None of which can wait until when we are ready or have enough time.

When busy, as so often we are, we fail to recognise or address our children's cues when they need us. This results in problems arising unnecessarily.

A proactive approach is recognising our children's cues and being flexible while having realistic expectations of them. Only we know what our children need and when and their level of maturity, and that is what we need to take into consideration at all times. So we can judge beforehand what kind of situation we are about to take our children into and decide whether or not it is age or stage appropriate for them.

If they cannot act their age, then we can be sure that the situation is not suitable for them.

We need to consider whether our expectations of our children are realistic or not.

For instance, on a long car journey, we can't realistically expect a young child to be quiet and sit still the whole time. We can, however, expect they will whinge and get bored, and the chances are, if we have more than one child, then we can also expect some squabbling with siblings along the way too.

This is being realistic. Young children have limited understanding. They have no concept of time or distance and are trying to manage the situation as best as an excited, energetic, frustrated child cooped up in a confined space can. Being bored, impatient, or over stimulated with excitement about the adventure that lies ahead is natural for a child. Sitting still and quiet, on the other hand, isn't!

If we can plan for their normal reaction by making regular stops for them to stretch their legs and take toilet breaks and engage positively and empathetically with them, we can make the journey a fun experience. Pointing out the scenery or playing games such as; count how many red cars you can see or spot the mini, and taking along activities such as colouring books and healthy treats to keep them satisfied and occupied helps. This way, they will be having so much fun and attention on the journey, they won't ever want to arrive at their destination.

TROUBLE SHOOT IN ADVANCE

It stands to reason that if everyday life affects our children, then major life changes will have a greater impact on them.

Change is unavoidable, all we can do is be prepared and be proactive, troubleshooting any potential problems in advance where possible.

Staying proactive everyday makes us more aware as parents. This way, we are able to notice the small changes in our children, preventing them from becoming big, dramatic changes.

This puts us in a better position to understand and anticipate how future events will impact and affect them, such as moving house, divorce, bereavement, illness, exams, starting a new school or childcare, etc.

We don't need an instruction manual to learn about our children, theory doesn't work in parenting practice, as every child and situation and family setup is unique. We just need routines so that we can become more aware and be willing to learn from past experiences. Ironically, our children are our best teachers. Everything you end up learning about parenting will come from your child, not a book or another parent.

Providing routine in our children's lives is the most proactive approach we can take. Routines help us to troubleshoot and understand their behaviour. When we provide our children with consistent routines and those routines become disrupted, we are able to account for certain behaviour. For example, if they have not slept well, we will know why they are emotional. Again, if they have not eaten their lunch, we'll understand why they are irritable. Then we can be more empathetic with how they are feeling and address whatever is preventing them from sleeping or eating normally and if possible, ensure it doesn't do so again in the future.

ROUTINE: THE HABIT OF ALL HAPPY, HEALTHY AND SUCCESSFUL PARENTS AND CHILDREN

Having worked with so many different children of all ages from all walks of life, I believe there's no such thing as a naughty child, a fussy eater, or a child who cannot sleep.

There are only children who lack routine, and therefore, develop their own habits in the absence of those routines.

Our children's routines are simply their everyday activities, such as going to bed or eating dinner at a certain time. Most children already follow some sort of routine, whether it's one that has been structured for them to follow, such as being put to bed at seven pm every evening, or one they have naturally adopted where they nap when they are tired around three pm each day. Both become habits ensuring adequate sleep.

Whether formed naturally or created by us for our children to follow, habits in life can work for or against us. For example, only eating junk food is an unhealthy habit, brushing our teeth is a healthy habit.

We can do them both every day without even thinking about it unless we choose consciously not to do them. This is hard work, anyone who's ever tried to go on a diet will tell you—the craving takes over. Breaking old habits can be a real struggle. Particularly if those habits provide us with pleasure or comfort, which most do. As human beings, we are all creatures of habit. We like the predictability and safety that our habits provide, like an old friend, we can rely on them to be there for us when we need them. As it's so hard to break old habits and resist temptation, it's best not to let our children develop unhealthy habits in the first place.

The problem then is not the habits themselves, it's whether they are healthy and helpful for our children or not.

If our children's habits are sporadic or dictated by the whims of our children's moods and emotions, they are not consistent routines. Routines should become automatic habits that should not depend on outside circumstances or feelings. What's important is understanding our children's habits and being able to influence or change them in order to steer them down the healthier, automatic highway.

To do this, it's essential we offer them alternative 'healthy habits' and the best way to do this is to provide them with a healthy, consistent routine.

Children especially like the predictability and stability that routines bring in an otherwise chaotic world. Lack of routine causes confusion, and that results in misbehaviour.

When our children don't know what is expected of them, when it's expected, and why we expect them to do something, they get confused, angry, and upset.

We might insist they go to bed at seven o'clock, but if that's not what they are used to doing, and they don't know why they must go to bed at that time all of a sudden, then they'll kick up a fuss. This emotional outburst will be even more severe if they are tired.

It's best to have a routine in place that they are used to, giving them a set of instructions that they can learn to follow until eventually, those instructions become an automatic habit.

CHILDREN NEED ROUTINE

Children just don't understand the reason why they are being overly emotional is because they are tired, hungry, or frustrated over something out of their control. Our role as parents is to identify their misbehaviour as a sign that they want us to take charge, direct them, or reassure them in some way, not to punish them for their behaviour.

This is when routines are useful because being young and uncertain on how to react or behave is scary enough without children having to worry about when they are going to eat their next meal or what time they need to go to bed. A regular routine takes care of all of that for them, and for us as parents too.

In the absence of routine, children can become labelled as naughty when they're actually hungry, tired, bored, restless, or attention seeking. We naturally assume that attention seeking behaviour is bad, but if our children are in constant need of our attention, then we need to identify this as the problem and find out why.

And again, routine helps us to do this because if we can rule out our children's unwanted behaviour as not being a result of hunger or tiredness, we now know there's another issue that needs our attention.

It's easy to overlook issues without a routine in place as we won't have a clue what is wrong with our child, making it easier to blame their behaviour as being the problem rather than finding out what problem is causing the behaviour.

That's because their behaviour is tangible, we can see, hear, or feel it even. So, if it's unwanted behaviour, the behaviour is the only problem we see, and we tend to react to their behaviour by trying to control or stop it with some form of punishment or threat.

ALLOWING THE MINOR TO BECOME THE MAJOR

Children may think they know what they want, but they are not mature or experienced enough to decide what is good or bad for them.

That's when they depend on us for guidance, not punishment.

No doubt they'll want to play all night long, but only because they don't understand the importance of rest in their lives and the impact lack of quality sleep has on them. When they fight their need to sleep, inevitably, they become over tired, and as a result, they become out of control and emotional with no understanding of why.

Lack of routine in their lives can make it easy for them to do their own thing based on how they are feeling at any particular time. But their feelings aren't reliable—routines are. We have to take a proactive approach to parenting and provide for their needs before they need them. Such as ensuring they go to bed at a consistent time every evening. This way, we limit and eventually prevent unwanted behaviour caused by tiredness.

If our children get enough time with us, adequate sleep, nutritious food, exercise, and plenty of recreation and love, then, those habits will obviously serve them better. Whereas a haphazard approach, left to their own devices, unsupervised, in an environment where they have complete control of what they do, staying up late, eating junk food in front of a screen is a recipe for disaster.

Now I'm not suggesting any of us allow that to happen intentionally, but letting our children stay up later than they should, occupied by a screen, can become a sneaky habit. Sometimes, for the sake of our sanity, we need a break, and the modern age babysitter, aka, the moving screen, is quick and convenient. It also delays the tantrum we know will erupt before bed, and in some cases, provides a lullaby for children to eventually drop off to so we don't have to face that dreaded situation.

But this catch 22 is a short-term solution to a longer-term problem.

WHAT'S IN IT FOR US?

Even if they fight it, all children need and like the predictability that routines offer, but it's also good for us parents. It's far easier and less stressful than fighting and arguing with our children, and it gives us the time for ourselves that we all need. When we all follow the same routine, harmony follows us. It gives the day order, and time serves a purpose in our lives. We become more organised and productive and able to plan ahead and pre-empt things ahead of time.

If we are trying to get some peace and quiet to unwind and relax, then we need to put our children to bed. That way, they can grow and recharge, while we enjoy our evening relaxing and recuperating. For that to work, we must establish a bedtime routine, or else we are making tomorrow an even harder day than today.

WHAT ROUTINES DO CHILDREN NEED?

As parents, we now know that we want routine, and our children need it, so let's give everyone what they want and need. But what routines exactly do our children need?

No matter how unique our children are, all children need exactly the same things to be happy, healthy, and successful, that is:

- Parents and carers who love them unconditionally and spend time with them, making them feel valued.
- Somewhere safe to call home.
- A routine which includes, recreational play time, sleep, exercise, love, and food.

It's about the small, consistent things that we do for our children that will make all the difference to their health, happiness, and success long term.

It's not about grand gestures, gadgets or gifts, fancy clothes, or holidays to exotic Islands riding camels across the desert. Although, these positive experiences and material possessions can and do make a difference to their wellbeing too. But ultimately, being a loving parent who offers a stable routine is the best gift that we can give our children today.

And it's the gift that keeps on giving because the sense of love, security, belonging, and comfort provided by a routine while young will stay with them as adults, helping them to feel more confident as people and happier in themselves.

THE U URSELF ROUTINE

As parents, we are responsible for our children's habits.

The U URSELF Routine is a routine that allows us to take charge and to feel Confident and Proactive as parents, guiding us in what we should be doing and when, just as much as our children.

And that's why U Time is part of the U URSELF Routine that I created.

It's a routine I used with my own children as well as helping other parents and their children that I've worked with over the years. It's tried and tested, and it works. That's why it's such an effective and valuable parenting tool, making it easy to deduce a lot from our children's behaviour when followed consistently on a daily basis.

Although I have created and used the U URSELF Routine with great success with my own children and have taught it to parents and children I have worked with over the past sixteen years as a Registered Childminder, Parent Coach, and Therapist. Only you know what is best for you and your child and your family as a whole. Each and every family has their own way of doing things and their own setup. Therefore, it's you yourself who will ideally decide the routines you want your child to follow. The U URSELF Routine is aptly called the U URSELF Routine because it's you yourself who will implement this routine and, ultimately, it's going to be you yourself who will make your child happy, healthy, and successful.

We don't have the space in this book to cover the U URSELF Routine itself (if you are interested in reading more about the U URSELF Routine in detail, then email me at emma@happychildcare.club or em@emmagrantauthor.com and I'll send you some more information, or alternatively, you can purchase my first book *The Confident Parent's Guide to Raising a Happy, Healthy & Successful Child*, which covers the routine in depth.); nonetheless; I'll offer a brief overview as follows.

It's one routine as a whole that comprises of seven different yet co-dependant aspects. In order for you to remember them, below is a useful mnemonic to help you, using the words 'You Yourself' abbreviated and spelt U URSELF. These combined are what I refer to as the U URSELF routine.

1. U
2. U
3. R
4. S
5. E
6. L
7. F

1 U time
2 Us time
3 Recreation
4 Sleep
5 Esteem
6 Love
7 Food

Those seven, separate, yet co-dependant routines combine into one solid tried and tested routine. Offering an outline of what every child needs and why, to be happy, healthy, and successful.

Individual in their own right, each are co-dependent on one another because it's pointless addressing our children's behavioural issues if we aren't addressing their sleep issues or other areas of their lives. As each aspect of our children's lives impacts one another, there's no point addressing your child's sleeping habits if you don't look at their exercise and recreational habits too. Like a missing piece of the puzzle, leaving out one area will fail to give us the whole picture. All the pieces or parts of the routine need to be collectively addressed at the same time.

We all do it, we focus on an area we feel is the problem and either buy a book dedicated to treating that problem or try to tackle that area head-on, failing to find the solution we are after.

We need to encompass our children's habits as a whole in all areas. Even those areas we are happy with that cause no issues.

They may be a good eater, but what are they eating and when?

This can all have an impact on their quality of sleep and be an underlying cause of their sleep problems.

The U URSELF routine will prove to be a useful, informative, motivational guide, providing ways in which you can effectively use the routine and the reasons why each aspect of the routine is important.

Even though much of it is common sense, having a motive or understanding the benefits of each aspect will give you the motivation and knowledge to stick to the routine, particularly when times become challenging.

If consistently followed, The U URSELF Routine is a reliable blueprint to guide you, but not if it's just on paper. You can read about it, and I can keep writing about it until we are blue in the face, but without taking action to implement it, it's worthless common knowledge. You have to be proactive in encouraging and following it with your child.

That's where most routines fail, our motivation wanes over time. When we lack motivation, we can never encourage our children to follow the routine, and without encouragement, routines are not carried out frequently enough to become habits.

Over time, with a consistent approach to the U URSELF routine, becoming over tired, starving hungry, bored or attention seeking will be eliminated most of the time as the routine endeavours to meet those needs in advance before it's too late.

By offering our children food before they are hungry or by putting them down for a nap just before they desperately need one, we help them to feel understood, cared for, and content. This prevents tears and tantrums for both parent and child, because trying to soothe an over tired baby to sleep is a very stressful time for all in earshot, so it's never a good idea to wait until it's too late.

Carve the path for your child to walk, or tread the hot coal's that follow, it's up to you.

TEACHING NOT PREACHING

Having said that, helping them to link cause and effect of their own actions and consequences is a useful learning opportunity. By explaining to them that the reason why they feel irritable is due to them not eating their food at lunch time, we help them to realise and understand their emotions and what causes them, so in future they can make better choices.

This way, instead of telling them off for their behaviour, we are educating them, and these lessons will serve them well throughout their lifetime. Being told off for their behaviour will not teach them anything other than they are wrong or naughty. This only serves to negatively affect their self-esteem, both now, and, if a constant source of discipline, in the future.

Instead of telling them off for not eating their food or for being irritable, we are alternatively helping them to understand how their actions have consequences and how those consequences can sometimes negatively affect them. Once they learn to link the two together, they'll be more inclined to eat their food next time, and there will be less aggravation all round.

SENSITIVITY

Recognizing and becoming sensitive to our children's needs and emotions is the only way to live in harmony with one another. As parents, nothing is more important than our children's happiness, yet work, the demands of the home, and our other relationships can sometimes take priority.

Juggling everything and everyone is stressful, but we have to remember that we are not the only ones finding life challenging sometimes. Everything's new to our children, and as they are emotionally immature, inexperienced, and constantly changing, this makes being young an unpredictable, scary, and confusing time for them.

If we provide a consistent, predictable routine in their lives, while empathizing and understanding the different stages that they are going through, we will successfully help them through the natural process of growing up.

Being aware of how our feelings and actions impact our children and being sensitive to any changes our children are faced with, such as starting school or moving house, is key.

As a counsellor and therapist, I have spent many hours with clients who have learnt their parents' behaviours to a tee. And most of these are unwanted behaviours or phrases they vowed they'd never use. We learn from our parents, so it stands to reason that our children will learn from us.

We have to be the person we want our child to become, but this is easier said than done!

Milestones such as our child starting school may be an anxious time for most parents, but these are major life changes for a small child. It's natural for them to feel apprehensive and scared, but we must try to remain calm and confident.

We don't want them to pick up on our fears and anxieties, but at the same time, we need to be understanding of what they are going through and available to support them, emotionally and physically.

PROACTIVE PREPARATION

Just as preparing for a journey in the car with our children, there are other times when we will need to plan ahead and prepare them. During life, changing events, such as starting school for the first time, we instinctively know that they will need comfort and reassurance. At these times, it is even more important to plan ahead and prepare ourselves and our children as much as possible. It is vital that we paint a positive picture beforehand when it comes to instances such as starting school or childcare and that we make sure they view any changes optimistically—as a positive, enjoyable experience. We can do this by telling them about all of the fun things they will get up to at school such as painting, play dough, and meeting new friends. Giving them something to look forward to builds excitement and helps them to understand what to expect. A proactive approach would also be taking them to visit the school environment to meet the teachers or carers before they actually start. Also, explaining to them why they are going there, when they are going, who else will be there, and what is expected of them when they are there will help them prepare. It is also a good idea to encourage them to ask any questions that they may have, such as where are the toilets? Or where are the Legos kept? Answering their questions and making it clear to them that we will be back to collect them after they have had a play helps to alleviate any fears or concerns that they may have. This preparation is essential before they start. School, nursery, or a childminders home are always full of new people and unknown experiences. At first, this can be daunting for any child, especially if they have never been left with anyone other than family members before. Being proactive means we expect that our children may not take to a new place or person straight away, we understand that we are asking them to go to an unknown place full of unfamiliar strangers. We may know it's a safe place, but our children may not, so we have to communicate this to them. This means being careful not to project or transfer our own anxieties, worries, or fears onto our children.

TRANSFERENCE

Our children pick up automatically on how we are feeling.

We may be telling them how much fun it's going to be at school, but if we are anxious and fretting over whether they will enjoy their first day or not, they'll sense it. Sensing our apprehension, they'll think there's something to be afraid of and that they too should be scared or worried.

Equally, if they excitedly run into school on their first day with not so much as a backward glance or goodbye, then that's okay too. They don't have to be happy or sad whenever we are not around.

Naturally, our children will not want to leave us. They love us and want to be with us as much as possible. We provide them with warmth, safety, comfort, and love, but if they can't wait to leave us and try out new things, it also shows what a great job we've done in helping them to feel secure and confident without us. We just have to allow them to settle into new experiences in their own way and in their own time. Providing we feel relaxed and optimistic about the changes, eventually, they will too. We just have to learn how to convey how we want them to feel. This can mean leaving our children, despite their kicking and screaming protests (all of which are incidentally staged for our benefit). If this is too much to bear, then finding someone else to drop them off until they get used to being left may help. Guaranteed, they will not perform as much in front of an emotionally detached audience, especially if they know that person is not going to give in to them or lavish them with attention.

As a childminder, I have seen it hundreds of times over the years—whenever I drop other people's children off to school, they skip in happily. Yet, if their parents take them, it's a full-on, award winning, Oscar performance of tears and tantrums.

Same child, same school, same time, same teachers, different carer dropping off.

KEEP A CLEAR PERSPECTIVE

This is stressful for everyone, but keeping a clear perspective of the situation and remembering that we are sending our children to school, and not evacuating them as some children once endured in the war, helps.

The worst thing we can do though, is show our children our own anxiety.

Being mindful of how our own emotions have an effect on our children and refusing to offer them any undue attention when overreacting is critical.

As children once ourselves, we may have felt insecure at times, and there may have been occasions that caused us apprehension, such as going to school, but they were our issues and feelings, not our children's.

Even if our children do display anxiety or emotions that are distressing, keeping in mind that children who experience the most separation anxiety are usually those whose parents are anxious about leaving them might remind us to relax. We need to be able to calm and reassure them that everything will be okay. We cannot do that if we are panicking or emotional ourselves.

We convey our fears by: continually kissing our children more than once when dropping them off, calling them back for a kiss or a cuddle once they have gone off to play, picking them up or carrying them in our arms and confirming how they are feeling with words like 'I know, I'm sorry, Mummy won't be long'.

This apologetic, fearful approach naturally upsets our children further and is made worse if a teacher or child carer has to physically prize our children off us as though taking them away against our will.

The good news is that once we stop feeling anxious, we can actually help to proactively prepare our children for change, and they will relax too. When our children are faced with change, not overreacting to their emotions, and taking steps to deal with our own anxiety and behaviours, will make them feel safer and more secure.

THE ENEMY OF PROACTIVITY

It's easy to get consumed and focus on our own grownup issues, and if we have doubts or fears and are not proactive in our approach, problems can paralyse us from taking any action at all. This condition is known as paralysis by analysis, it is when we become plagued with indecision and get caught up in a state of overthinking an issue. Then, instead of dealing with it, we worry about it, often resulting in the issue never getting dealt with or resolved effectively.

All parents worry or feel anxious on a daily basis.

When it comes to our children, we can worry about everything and anything as we deliberate on what they should eat, how they are progressing at school, and how to deal with their unwanted behaviour.

This can become a constant source of stress for most of us as we feel we must instantly sort everything out the right way. Understandably, this puts pressure on us, making it difficult to think straight and making decision making impossible sometimes. All of this responsibility can weigh heavy on us and overwhelm us, especially if there are pressures on us from others such as teachers or spouses adding to the problem itself.

Undoubtedly, all of this deliberation and failure to make important decisions undermines our self-confidence, which complicates matters more than actually dealing with them. Taking decisive action and doing something, even if that action is not the right action to take, sets the solutions to problems in motion. When we put ourselves out there, answers find us, but when we procrastinate or are fearful of making the wrong choices and take no action to solve an issue, this not only leads to a lack of confidence in our own parenting abilities but prevents us from finding a suitable outcome for our children's problems—consequently creating more of our own.

TAKING ACTION

The only solution is for us to proactively take action to prevent or deal with problems, rather than Auto Pilot Parent when things go wrong.

This empowers us to handle our children's behaviour and their reactions to situations and puts us in a better position to help them to deal with their emotions without getting caught up in our own.

We can aim for damage limitation, but we can't wrap our children up in cotton wool and prevent them ever getting hurt or upset in life, that's all a necessary part of the learning process for their growth and development. Children need to encounter challenging situations and learn how to deal and respond appropriately to them, which primarily they will learn from us. If they see us handling things confidently, calmly, and collectedly, then their own behaviour will be a lot calmer too and will eventually start to reflect our own.

They will still misbehave as part of growing up and testing their boundaries, and there will be a hundred and one ways in which we can deal with it. Usually, though, we become so caught up and involved in the behaviour itself and how to deal with it that we end up doing very little to positively change it, and as a result, we just end up worrying about it instead.

Sometimes, taking a proactive approach can mean stepping back and away from the problem itself. Then, when we are less involved in the emotional side, we can start to narrow down a couple of options that we could take, and then take assertive action.

As an example, we may find ourselves deliberating over several possible schools that we could send our children to. When faced with such an important decision, choosing the right school could seem more daunting than it really is. Once we relax, step back, and think clearly, the decision usually rests on only one of two possibilities, and that is the way with most problems.

It's having the clarity to narrow things down and knowing that even if we make a wrong choice, we can feel reassured that we can always change course if we are taking our children in the wrong direction. Being proactive eliminates doubt, so even if we think we might be wrong with our choices and later it turns out we were, then that's better than never knowing and not taking any action and allowing others to take the lead. What we will likely find when we take this approach is that we can never really make a wrong decision anyway, just a different one.

DOUBTS FEARS & TEARS

I myself removed my children halfway through primary school from a Welsh Medium School to an English Medium School (nothing to do with the language may I add). Initially, when I chose the Welsh School, I was happy with that decision. A few years later, that decision no longer felt like the right thing for my children, leaving me to make the proactive decision of changing their schools. A lot of parents felt the same way as me at the time and also wanted to remove their children, but they didn't, as they were fearful how it would affect them. I, on the other hand, feared how keeping them there would affect them, but it was a decision I needed help with, so I proactively involved my children in the decision-making process every step of the way. This took a lot of the pressure off me to make the decision and gave them a choice. My daughter was keen to change schools, my son, however, was not so keen. I asked them to draw up a list of the pros and cons for staying in their old school and moving to the new school. Both had more pros for moving and more cons for staying put. The decision was made instantly based on those lists. I didn't dwell on it or give them time to worry about the consequences, I took immediate action. Today, they are now in High School, but they have never regretted moving schools, and the only effects it had on them were positive. They've made great best friends that otherwise they would never have met and are both confident and sociable. And despite joining a new school midway through a term, their academic ability has soared. Children are much more resilient than we give them credit for, it's us as parents who have the doubts, fears, and tears, not our children.

PARENTAL INTUITION

The initial idea to change schools came from my own parental intuition. I could have taken the easy option and ignored what I felt. I could have found many excuses to keep them in their old school, but that would have kept me reactive as a parent, not proactive. I probably would have been complaining to the school over issues that I was unhappy with for years and would have always wondered, what if they had gone to a different school?

Proactivity quashes regrets before they fester.

Feeling confident to take action comes from that parental intuition that we all have which arises from knowing and loving our children. This insight is invaluable to tune into as it helps us to know how our children will respond to certain people, events, or situations in advance. This gives us time to take the necessary steps in order to avoid situations turning out undesirably.

Fortunately, this proactive approach arising from instinct or intuition is something we naturally do as parents most of the time anyway.

Although my husband and I made the right choice in moving our children to a different school, and both of our children excelled in their new school, none of us regret them having gone to the old school. My children also made some great friends there too, and they learnt how to speak Welsh fluently at a young age and how to change and adapt to new circumstances and form new relationships, all invaluable skills to learn at a young age.

We all learn from experimentation and experience.

As parents, we need to accept that we won't always make the right choices or decisions all of the time. That's okay, because we can and will learn from all of them, good or bad, along the way.

As long as we keep moving, we will make progress and rid ourselves of this paralysis by analysis. By doing what we can, we can feel confident in the knowledge that we are always doing our best.

We will then be free to relax, knowing that we cannot control everything that happens to our children.

This is a good thing, because we cannot learn everything for them, there will be times when they will have to learn for themselves, and often the hard way. The most proactive thing that we can all do as parents is to decide today to stop worrying about our children's behaviour, education, health, happiness, safety, success, or whatever else is worrying us at the moment, and take action to do something about it.

We can start today by doing the following 'Worry Busting' exercise. This simple technique helps alleviate a certain degree of worry straight away and helps us to gain a clearer perspective, focusing more on solutions rather than problems.

THE WORRY BUSTER TECHNIQUE

- First, think about something that is worrying you at this moment regarding your child.
- Now, write down all the reasons why it is worrying you, and note how worrying about it has helped the situation or how it has made it worse.
- Then, work out how long you have been worrying about it, and decide how much longer you want to keep on worrying about it.
- Next, write a list of all the possible ways that you can try to help solve the problem or make it less of a worry. Brainstorm as many ideas as you can think of, regardless of how unrealistic they may sound at first.
- Now, choose one way that you can take action on the problem today.
- Finally, go and take some action and do something to change the situation now.

Can't find a solution right now? Then just decide to relax and step back and accept, for now, the way things are.

Clear your mind of the problem and do something else until a solution comes to mind. Busy yourself with chores or exercise and let the solution bubble away in the back of your mind unhindered by you.

You've proactively looked at the issue by doing the 'Worry Busting Technique'. Now the only thing you can change is to stop worrying about something you cannot change because if there is nothing you can do about it, then why waste time and energy worrying?

Worrying will not help or change anything. After all, most of what we worry about never actually happens anyway, and if we are doing all that we can do right now, then there is no need to worry about anything else.

COMFORT BLANKET

As Proactive Parents, we don't want to add to our children's worries either. We want to offer them comfort and reassurance in difficult times, so our words and actions need to wrap them up like a snuggly comfort blanket of love. Just being aware of when our children need us the most and our presence should be enough.

This can be easy to overlook though. Often, the things that our children get upset and worry about can seem insignificant to us with our real grownup issues to deal with.

At two in the morning, we may know that there are no monsters under the bed, but a three-year-old may not. At those times, particularly when we are tired and angry, we can unintentionally miss the opportunity to give them an explanation, hug or a kiss, and to make them feel better, especially if they are behaving undesirably. Yet this is when they are crying out for help, and yes, attention. The monsters under the bed may not be the real problem, but if we brush them back under the bed, we'll never know. Ironically, it's those times when they misbehave and don't understand their own emotions that we end up getting upset and angry with them, when all they really want and need is a cuddle.

Understanding and being sensitive to how they are feeling is not always easy, we may offer words of reassurance when they are scared such as: 'Don't be silly there's nothing to be afraid of' but this does little to comfort them when they are feeling afraid. Our children need to feel like we take their concerns seriously, and that we empathize with them.

Especially older children who need reassurance long after they have discarded their comfort blanket. When their best friend has just moved away or their first love has just dumped them for someone else, they may quite literally think and feel that their whole world has come to an end, and we can unwittingly exacerbate that further if we discount their feelings when they turn to us for support. Their drama is as real as going over our overdraft the day after payday, so we shouldn't treat it as a joke.

A worry is worry, regardless. As Proactive Parents, we need to ask ourselves how we would feel if we had just lost our best friend or the love of our life had just left us?

We may feel frustrated at our clumsy toddler for accidentally dropping their ice cream on the floor, but how do you think they are feeling?

Do we want to make them feel even worse by telling them off and getting angry, adding to their sadness over losing something that they really wanted? Dropping our ice cream on the floor, breaking friends, and being dumped hurts, regardless of our age or duration of the relationship. We don't want our children to feel that their dramas and accompanying emotions are insignificant to us. It's important they feel that we really do care and that we understand what they are going through, no matter how young or old they are. By remaining sensitive to how they are feeling and allowing them the chance to experience their emotions, happy or sad, then providing we are on hand with the tissues and tubs of ice cream to proactively make it all better when things do go wrong, we can prevent them getting upset with us and lessen their distress.

THE HOW-TO PART

Hopefully by now, the first part of this book will have helped you to realise the importance of habitual routines in your child's life.

Although I'm pretty sure you knew that already.

Now it's time to address the how-to part. This is the hard part most of us struggle with or overlook. When we have avoided tackling routines for so long, we normally get to a breaking point of enough is enough!

Then, when we do finally decide to introduce a routine, we become impatient and tend to dive straight in, telling our children what we want them to do and demanding they do it without thinking things through beforehand.

Yet the proactive approach is always one of thoughtful planning and pre-empting. Our children's need for routine, coupled with their deep-down desire to please us, is good news for us parents. It means we are halfway there to implementing a successful routine already. But don't get excited too quickly, that doesn't mean they are going to make it any easier for us. So, let's give ourselves and our children the best chance of success by thinking about it first.

This book is independent in its own right; however, as I've already said, I do have another book which compliments it called *The Confident Parent's Guide to Raising a Happy, Healthy & Successful Child* which enhances the overall proactive approach to parenting. If you've already read that book, then the rest of this chapter will be familiar to you, so feel free to jump forward to chapter two—Auto Pilot Parenting.

If not, this gives us time to make a cuppa, settle back down comfortably, and plan our approach carefully. It's the calm before the storm, so please don't skip this bit and rush through to the Managing Unwanted Behaviour or Making the Perfect Child section of the book. There's going to be plenty of opportunities to take action, for now, just relax, gather some energy, put your feet up, and enjoy as you contemplate when and how to start.

WHEN & HOW TO START A ROUTINE

I'm sure you're eager to begin implementing routine in your child's life by now.

Before we charge straight in, there's some pointers to consider first.

Twelve points to be precise, which are as follows.

1. Start Now
2. Be Patient
3. Be Understanding
4. No Punishment or Reward
5. Big up the Benefits
6. Warnings and Reminders
7. Stick to your Guns
8. Difficulties and Disruptions

1.   START NOW

It's never too soon to introduce routine in our children's lives, the younger they are the better. Starting healthy eating, sleeping, and activity routines from birth is best but not essential.

Starting now and starting as we mean to go on is the proactive parent's motto for success!

Establishing routines early on integrates them as a normal and natural part of our children's lives. Even if you haven't given birth yet, preparations and decisions concerning routines can start now, the earlier the better.

Babies adapt quickly and are more accepting of routines than older children because:

- They know no other way and haven't had the chance to form bad habits.
- Routines help them to make sense of their chaotic new world.
- They are unable to independently meet their constant needs.
- They are unable to verbally communicate their needs to us.

We can find it difficult to know what they want, when, and why. Especially if we are new to the world of parenting, but with a routine, we can work it out.

Don't wait and put off a routine until you feel like they are old enough to understand. A six- week old baby is more inclined to sleep alone in their own bed and accept and understand a bedtime routine, than a six- year old that's used to co-sleeping and going to sleep at whatever time we retire to bed.

Having said that, if you have a six -year old and not a baby, it's still better to set a routine now, whatever their age, rather than not at all. The specifics of routines will always change over time anyway, but it's easier to change their routines than it is to suddenly create them from nowhere.

Our children can easily adapt to going to bed an hour later as they get older. But try telling a seven-year-old to go to bed an hour earlier than they are used to because of a new routine we want to start and we'll find this will be just as much of a challenge for us as it will be for our children.

2.   BE PATIENT

In the beginning, implementing any new routine will require patience, energy, and understanding on everyone's part.

The secret to successful routines will largely depend on how patient we are at carrying them out and how we encourage our children to follow them.

It means showing unconditional love, even when they refuse to eat the dinner that we've lovingly cooked for them, and giving them enough time to practice getting used to their new bedtime routine by preparing them for bed a little earlier in the evening.

Trying to introduce more than one new routine at a time is going to be difficult for any child to understand, like, or accept to begin with.

Start by introducing one new routine at a time, and start as you mean to go on (remember our motto?).

We may feel frustrated with our children when they won't go to bed when we tell them to or whenever they refuse to eat their dinner, however, we still have to be patient in how we handle the situation.

It's tempting to expect them to change overnight because we want them to, but children won't change if we force or rush them.

Routines present opportunities to learn new and better ways of doing things, but they are best carried out in a calm, relaxed, and patient manner. Telling them off or rushing them to eat their meal is unproductive. The priority is on our children eating a well-balanced, overall diet and enjoying the mealtime experience. Not making them sit at the table trying to force them to eat their vegetables or clear their plate.

Each child and circumstance are different, but most, if not all, children will get used to routines when they can digest them in their own time.

Big disclaimer here though, no routine should become more important than our children's health or happiness. The whole point of routine is to help our children, not to punish them in any way. Sometimes, it may take a while for them to understand that routines are for their own good. We just have to learn how to be patient and understanding to how they are feeling until they do.

3.   BE UNDERSTANDING

Trying to understand that new routines can seem unfair to our children and realising that they have only developed their current habits because we have let them can be difficult.

By allowing our children to _____ (fill in the blank with whatever you have allowed your child to do), for example, bed share for the last six years with you, then acknowledging that, intentionally or unintentionally, you have allowed it to become part of their normal routine (and now they know no other way) is a vital first step in changing things. It's a habit we've either allowed, created, or continued, or how else did it last so long?

Knowing this, we have to expect some resistance to change, understanding before we begin that introducing a new routine is not going to be an easy transition for anyone. Particularly not for our children. We might know what we are trying to achieve and see the bigger picture, but they won't.

We know we are not changing their routine to hurt or punish them. Still, we need to be mindful of their feelings and empathetic in our approach without feeling sorry for them. We can still let them know that we understand how they are feeling about the sudden changes and can empathize, but we don't want to sympathize. What we are asking them to do is not something horrible—we are introducing routines for their own good out of love. That doesn't mean that they are going to feel good about them in the beginning though. If we have co-slept with our child for the last six years but now would like them to move into their own bed in their own room, then we need to understand how they might feel.

In their mind, we're telling them to move from the shared, warm, safe comforts that they have always known to the cold, lonely, dark, unknown room across the landing. Understandably, this new routine would upset them and seem more like a punishment for growing up, leading to protests or regressive behaviours such as bed wetting or clinginess. Their behaviour toward the changes would not be intended to upset us for moving them into their own room, though. Rather, they would be a normal reaction to change and to feeling afraid, anxious, or unsettled. Any regressive behaviours are simply their way of showing us that they still need us or are simply a coping mechanism to return to that time when they felt protected. Those moments of unsettled or regressive behaviours require reassurance from us that everything will be okay. To do this, we need to be understanding, dispelling any fears they may have in a calm and confident manner whilst still communicating to them that it's not a bad change in circumstances, it's just different!

4.   ROUTINE PUNISHMENT

If we scold them whenever our children fail to comply, then we run the risk of making routines look more like punishments. We shouldn't display our anger when they don't follow their routines. We wouldn't be angry over them refusing cake that we offer out of love, and it's the same with their routines. They are a token of our love, and our children will come to love them also if we never use them as punishment.

It's common to hear parents threaten their children with:

'If you don't behave, you'll go to bed early' or 'If you don't eat your dinner there will be no dessert.'

Since when has going to bed or eating dinner been a punishment?

For us parents, eating and sleeping are usually the best parts of our day!

We want our children to look forward to returning to bed after a long day just as we do and to enjoy their dinner as much as dessert.

If we threaten them with bed as a punishment or bargain with them to eat their dinner before dessert, then they'll come to think that going to bed is a punishment and dessert is a reward for enduring nasty vegetables!

5. BIG UP THE BENEFITS OF ROUTINE

Instead, it's best to explain the benefits of routine to our children in an age appropriate way that they'll understand so they know that we are trying to help them, not punish them in any way.

This way, they are more likely to cooperate and adjust to their routines. If we can point out and prove the benefits of a routine and explain how it's a natural, necessary part of every child's day in ways they understand, then life will be a lot easier.

Some children will be motivated by reward and benefits, if your child is one of those children, then highlight the benefits of following their routine. Others are motivated by not losing out or by not being negatively affected by their actions. If your child is one of those types, explain to them the negative consequences of not following a routine. This will help them to avoid those negative consequences.

We are not trying to make our children feel guilty or scared in any way, just helping them to associate their behaviour and actions (or inactions as the case may be) with the consequences. But keep it positive and big it up at all times, the benefits to any routine should always outweigh the consequences of not following the routine.

This is something they may be unable to do alone. For instance, each time they stay up late at night and struggle to get out of bed for school the next morning, we can point out that they are tired because they went to bed late, and if they go to bed on time in the future then they will wake up a lot easier, feeling a lot better.

Or if they've refused to eat dinner and a couple of hours later become hungry, irritable, or emotional, we can point out that their feelings are a result of hunger, and next time, they will be a lot happier if they eat their dinner.

It's a good idea to keep a balance between the positive reasons for following the routine and the negative reasons for not. This means, if they refuse to go to bed, we can point out the positive reasons why they should and highlight the negatives of staying awake, so a typical example could sound like this:

'Go to sleep now, Sam, or else you will be too tired to play with your friends at nursery tomorrow and that won't be any fun. You need plenty of sleep to give you energy so you can climb that big climbing frame when you go to the park with Granddad in the afternoon too. So, the sooner you go to sleep, the quicker tomorrow will come and you can show him how high you can climb. But you won't be able to if you are too tired.

It may seem like a long-winded way to say:

'Go to sleep!'

But it's the quickest and most effective way in the long run.

Highlighting the positives and negatives encourages our children to want to follow routines a lot more than just telling them to comply or else. Providing an explanation helps them to know exactly why it benefits them and why we want them to go to sleep.

When they understand the benefits to them, routines then make sense.

6.   WARNING & REMINDERS

Even when children are familiar with and understand the benefits of their routines, if absorbed in play or watching their favourite TV programme, they won't welcome the interruption those routines bring. Those things they enjoy doing will always outweigh the benefits of going to bed to sleep. Unfortunately, that's life! They have to get used to it, but we can make it easier for them to accept. The best way to do that is to give them plenty of warnings and reminders. The worst way is to suddenly end their fun.

For example, if their bedtime is at seven and as soon as the clock turns, we abruptly say to them:

'Come on time for bed now!'

This can be an unwelcome surprise.

We need to gradually prepare our children with warnings and reminders first. Letting them know fifteen to ten minutes beforehand that it's nearly time for bed gives them the chance to mentally and physically prepare themselves.

Young children have no concept of time, it's pointless saying they have ten minutes then forget to warn them until the time is up. Instead, we need to keep on reminding them at intervals, starting with:

1. Ten minutes—'Pack away your toys now, it's almost time for bed.'
2. Five minutes—'Go and brush your teeth before bed.'
3. Two minutes—'Let's have a kiss, ready for bed.'
4. One minute—'Jump into bed for your bedtime story.'

Or at mealtimes:

1. Ten minutes—'Let's turn the TV off, food's almost ready to eat.'
2. Five minutes—'Wash your hands before eating.'
3. Two minutes—'Sit at the table, food's coming.'

Preparation is vital in helping children wind down and feel ready for when the time finally arrives. Communication doesn't have to be verbal though. For babies, words won't be able to prepare them, but having before bed routines, such as bath, massage, cuddle, and bottle will.

7. STICK TO YOUR GUNS

Our children may not always welcome their routines with open arms, but we know how important they are to our children's overall wellbeing. That knowledge gives us the confidence to stand firm and stick to our guns when conflict arises.

I've met lots of children who lack routine in their daily lives, but I've yet to meet one child who hasn't benefited from some sort of daily routine. I assure you, if you hang in there and stick to your guns, everyone will benefit.

This means, often, you'll be hanging on a thread as your patience frays, but if seven o clock is bedtime, then our children should go to bed at seven every evening. Routine is all about doing the same things, at the same times. However, there's no need to get neurotic if their bedtime is seven pm and they are still brushing their teeth at seven fifteen.

It's normal for children to stall going to bed.

They all mysteriously get this sudden urge to discuss events that happened in their day. Conveniently, these important matters can never wait, even though they've forgotten to mention them for the last six hours or more!

To resolve such stalling, all we need to do is to let them know calmly that in future they will need to get ready for bed a little earlier, allowing them more time to chat about their day or brush their teeth.

They may be a little more reluctant to chat about insignificant things when they realise it'll take up the last few minutes of their playtime or take away time for their bedtime story in the evening.

Alternatively, you may find that your child is not dawdling deliberately to stay up later but are taking their time because they are tired and may actually need to go to bed a bit earlier in future.

In any case, if we expect our children to stick to their routines, we have to stick to them too. If we fall short in one area, say, finishing work late, delaying our children's meal, then the chances are, not only our children's mealtime routine will be late but their bedtime routine also. Like a domino effect, a change in one can have a knock-on effect to every other routine.

8.   DIFFICULTIES & DISRUPTIONS

There will always be occasions when things don't go to plan—when it's inevitable that routines will be disrupted or difficult to stick to. Even well-established routines become disturbed at times, for all sorts of reasons.

Sometimes, it's sensible to allow them to be relaxed, but only with good reason, as this can result in our children acting out of character.

Sickness, late nights, holidays, celebrations, bereavement, starting school/day care, visitors, and general problems at home can all have an impact on our children's routines, causing havoc in the process. Some interruptions to routine such as accidents or unexpected visitors are unavoidable and can't be anticipated or planned for. But if we do know in advance that a visitor to the home is going to interfere with our child's routine or a future event is about to unfold, then we can proactively warn them in advance while making adjustments to minimise disruption. Disruptions are inevitable from time to time, although inconvenient, we can know this and can understand what's going on. We can also feel okay about the situation, but our children may not. Routines directly affect them, so they can feel confused, tired, hungry, or overwhelmed, and worst of all, powerless over what happens to them.

These disruptions should always be taken into consideration, especially if our children's behaviour has become disruptive as a result. Understanding the cause of our children's behaviour can help us to deal with the behaviour more appropriately and effectively.

Whatever the disruptions to routine may be, the most important thing we can do is settle them back into their usual routine as soon as possible, or create a new one if needs be.

This can be difficult if the disruptions affect us too.

We may not always have the strength to persevere if we are not feeling good. For example, if bereavement has caused a routine to become unsettled or neglected, then chances are, we will also be affected by this in some way.

SINGLE PARENTS

I have found it is not uncommon for parents who have recently split up to turn to their children for comfort. Often, allowing them to stay up later or bed share with them. This is usually justified by thinking that their children are feeling insecure and need them. This is right, they probably do, but in most cases, the truth is, the newly single parent needs the child to need them as they are feeling rejected or sad. There's nothing wrong with needing some love when we are feeling low, as long as we know that's what's happening and why.

And understand that it's not our children's fault when we find happiness again and decide we no longer want them to stay up late or bed share with us and try to change that.

Now, I'm not picking on single parents here. I admire them most (I myself grew up in a one parent family without my Mum) as they have to do all this parenting routine stuff alone, often with little or no support. But I couldn't help noticing that when some parents split up, a competitive game can ensue between the two.

They say children always suffer when parents use them in their games (really, this is a game no one ever really wins), but I've found, children are the only ones who really ever win at this game as they learn how to play one parent off against the other. Parents wanting to be the 'best parent' often give in to their children. That normally means allowing them to stay up late, eat treats, and have gifts for no reason. Routine especially falls by the wayside when the absent parent who only has limited time such as weekends to spend with their child wants to 'make the most of their time together'.

The poor parent who spends most of their time with the child, tirelessly providing a routine, then has to suffer the rest of the time with a tired child. A child who often prefers their other parent as they do more fun things and give them what they want. If you are at the receiving end of this from an ex- partner and parent to one of your children, then, as a proactive parent, you have to address it. This is a stressful situation as the other parent may use this against you. You may understandably worry they might deliberately go against your wishes and flout your routines as a way of getting you back for past hurts.

It's likely they may try, on the other hand. They may be totally unaware of the problems they are causing and may well apologise and try to help you. They may have only been doing it out of a genuine, misguided love for your child. And their motives may innocently stem from wanting to spend happy time with them or as a result of them trying to compensate out of guilt for not being around as much anymore.

In either instance, your child's health and happiness is what's most important. If in any doubt, proactively pass this book onto the other parent so you are both on the same page.

9.   KEEPING IT REAL

Certain routines and their timing will be personal to each individual child within a family. One child may be younger, making their bedtime different from their older siblings, and this is where difficulties can lie.

They may resist being the only one going to sleep early, and we can't force them to sleep. But we still have to insist on them following their bedtime routine. We have to tell them to go to their room to sleep and make sure that they are in bed at the right time.

As long as they stay in their bed, whether they sleep or not, is ultimately up to them (but don't worry, using this same approach every night and going to bed at the same time will eventually be all the cue they need to fall asleep naturally, in fact, they'll come to expect it!).

The younger the child, the easier and quicker this will be. It's the same with mealtimes, if they don't want to eat, then all we can do is offer them a healthy, nutritious meal and let them decide to eat it or not. We can't actually do it for them or force them to do anything. We just need to provide the routines for our children to follow as best they can, then, our part as loving, responsible, Proactive Parents is done.

10.   REVIEW ROUTINES

Over time, our children's needs will change. If a routine has stopped working, then these changes will need to be reflected in their routines. A three-year-old will naturally need less sleep than when they were a baby, and a ten-year-old may not be tired at six pm anymore.

By reviewing routines regularly, we can see what's still suitable and what's not. This way, knowing we are doing the right thing, for the right reasons, at the right time means we can feel confident and stick to the routines we have set, even when our children try to change them.

We have parental responsibility over our children for good reason. Change or abolish their routines they may try, but the onus is on us to stay strong and persevere.

11.   STAY STRONG & PERSERVERE

We shouldn't give up and let our children's defiance toward their routines discourage us. By persevering and keeping routines going regardless, whether our children follow them or not, we provide the regularity and certainty that they need in their life. Unquestionably, with practice and patience, routines soon become habits for most children, even the reluctant ones.

Children can, however, be very creative in their approach to flouting new routines, and also very wearing and persistent. I remember my own two little ones complaining at bedtime about the children who were younger than them, playing outside in the street and questioning me why they had to go to bed while the sun was still shining?

Using guilt as their preferred tool of negotiation, they protested:

'I don't want to go to bed, it's not fair, the sun is still out.'

But I was confident that keeping to their bedtime routine was good for them. That's how I managed to remain calm and stay strong and persevere.

It was hard, though, I must admit. But had I felt guilty and uncertain that what I was doing was unfair, I may have succumbed and given in, allowing them to stay up a little later.

That would have been a BIG mistake!

If we succumb to our children's guilt trips and move the goal posts just once, then we can expect them to move them even further the next time as they try to find out how far they can push things in their favour.

Guaranteed, next time, they will use that as their trump card. If we do succumb, we have to prepare ourselves to be subjected to most children's favourite phrase, you know the one that makes most parents cringe in annoyance at themselves of: 'It's not fair, you let me yesterday, why not today?'

To which, no parent can ever find a justifiable explanation.

So, we either end up giving into them once again, creating another unwanted habit that's hard to break or, we become annoyed and upset with ourselves for giving in to them in the first place, resulting in a no win for us parents but possible triumph for our little ones! Once we've allowed something once, there's usually no going back.

REVELLING IN THE RESULTS

That's why it's best to persevere and stay strong from the outset. If we can persevere with routines until we get the results we want, then life will become much easier for ourselves as well as our children. Other parents and their children (such as those playing outside at bedtime) may take a different approach.

And that's fine for them. After all, they're the ones who will be responsible for their own children's health and wellbeing and managing their own children's behaviour. But you will be responsible for your children, no one else's. Focusing on the most beneficial, proactive approach that's suitable for you and your child is always best. This, I may add, is not the easiest approach initially. But I promise, long term, you'll be revelling in the results. Keeping consistent is key, routines are then fair and make sense. And when they make sense to our children, the sun may have his hat on, but our children will try to sleep anyway!

12.   BE PREPARED

As the old adage goes 'No plan is a plan to fail'. So, let's be prepared with a plan of action. The U URSELF routine is the best plan I've found to work with the children I've cared for, but feel free to find your own.

Whatever routine you use, there'll be times along the way (likely when you're scraping a meal you've spent hours lovingly preparing into the bin! Or when your unappreciative child is moaning about an activity or outing you've arranged for them as part of Us time together) when you will wonder why you are bothering.

This is perfectly normal; most routines are basic and straight forward, but that's not to say they will always be easy.

If you are prepared for those times and stick with it and are consistent in your approach, you will soon see why you bothered, and you will be glad that you did!

We just have to take it one day at a time. No matter how much we prepare our children or no matter how prepared we think we are, we will still find implementing routines difficult at times. That's why we need to choose a time to introduce any new routines when we are feeling both mentally and physically strong and determined. It's easier for us to give up and give in to our children if we are tired or frustrated ourselves.

Parents constantly tell me that the reason why they gave up on a routine was because of their children's resistant, unwanted behaviour toward the routine. Whatever the particular issues that they were having, whether it was eating or sleeping problems, what they are saying is that they found their children's behaviour too much for them to handle. It's a scary thought that a child can have that much control over an adult, but it's very common.

Unfortunately, every time we give in to our children, we hand them over a little more power each time and create a habit that's hard for them to break. But more than that, giving in to them also means any effort made previously in trying to establish a routine was all in vain and a total waste of time, tears, effort, and energy.

Fortunately, the parents I know who have introduced their children to the U URSELF Routine and have followed the suggestions set out here in this book tell me that their children love the new routine and are happier, healthier, and more successful as a result.

And why wouldn't they be, it's to benefit them, after all.

What child wouldn't want more time, understanding, love, and attention?

And what parent wouldn't want that for their child?

I'm not here to advise you on specifics such as what time your child should go to bed, that's for you to decide. What's important is understanding our children's habits and being able to influence or change them in order to steer them down the healthier automatic highway. But more importantly, is understanding our own habitual ways of behaving and avoiding auto pilot parenting, which is what we'll address next.

CHAPTER 2:
AUTO PILOT PARENTING

THE ONLY WAY WE CAN tell if we are taking the right type of action is if we are consciously aware of how we are acting, or reacting as the case may be.

There's a difference between:

- Being proactive, aware, and learning from our mistakes; and
- Being reactive, repeatedly making the same mistakes, and being unaware we are making them.

The first is proactive parenting, the second is Auto pilot parenting. In the latter case, there's no point taking action if it's the wrong type of action.

OUR ABILITY TO RESPOND

We all have the ability to respond to our children and situations as we choose. The problem is, we aren't always aware that we are not choosing but reacting in the heat of the moment when caught up in emotion or busyness. Even if our children always behaved well, our lives would still have problems, just different ones caused by different people.

It's true that our children's unwanted behaviour is the stimulus to our stress sometimes, but how we choose to respond to their behaviour is up to us. It's our responsibility. Break that word down, and it literally means our ability to respond. We can perpetuate the problem by fighting fire with fire and shouting, smacking, or punishing our children in some other way, or we can look at changing our reactions and responding differently. No matter how proactive we are, our children will still get upset and misbehave. Equally, there will be times when we still get angry and upset at our children, but generally, when our lives are going well and we feel happy, then what our children do or don't do doesn't negatively affect us, and if it does, we are able to deal with it appropriately and rationally.

BLAME GAME

Resolving conflict is difficult when we believe our children's behaviour is to blame for how we are feeling, or when our children feel we are against them. Both sides end up playing the blame game. But we are never against our children, and they are not the reason why we react a certain way. Our responses to their behaviour are usually automatic. When it comes to managing their unwanted behaviour, we adopt the same methods of auto pilot parenting out of habit without questioning our effectiveness. We've simply developed a bad habit of reacting to our children, and our children have developed a bad habit of responding to us. Often, parents and children aren't consciously aware of what they are doing or saying or the impact they are having.

We can assume so much this way about one another that's simply not true and label behaviour as wrong or naughty, when really, it's just misunderstood. Our child spilling a drink on the carpet is not naughty, it's more likely an innocent accident, yet out of frustration, we may shout at them for it. Especially if we have a nice new cream carpet that's now covered in blackcurrant juice!

Responding in the heat of the moment when emotions are high is an Auto Pilot reaction. We're not noticing our own behaviour toward our children because it's become an automatic response to shout or smack and to focus only on what they are doing wrong. These responses are a reflection of how we are thinking or feeling as opposed to how our children are behaving. For example, what if they spilt water on an old, black carpet? Would our reaction be as severe as the cream carpet covered in blackcurrant juice?

When we become reactive instead of proactive, we shout at our children because they are shouting, or we smack them because they have hit another child. When we behave the same way as our children, we reinforce the behaviours we are trying to stop. All we really want to do is prevent upset and make the situation better but end up antagonising and adding to the problem instead of solving it.

Luckily, once we've become aware of our own behaviour, we can break this auto pilot habit. Having a clear perspective of our own motives and how, when, and why we set rules or react to our children helps.

CLASSIC AUTO PILOT PARENTING BLAME GAME

Sometimes, this is easier to see in others than ourselves. I remember at my daughter's gymnastics class when she was younger that I noticed another Mum I knew being short tempered with her children.

She'd been so upset, she was on the verge of bursting into tears. When I had asked what had made her feel this way, she'd replied, 'My Kids!'

They had wanted a sandwich before gymnastics but were eating it too slow. Then, one of them didn't like the shoes she had told them to wear, making her feel fed up because she didn't want to go to gymnastics anyway. It would've been easier for her, she said, to stay at home after the horrible day she'd had at work.

This was a classic case of Auto Pilot Parenting—her children were not to blame for how upset she was feeling but a confrontation at work. In her angry state, she couldn't see this initially. As we chatted, she realised eating a sandwich too slow or disliking a pair of shoes wouldn't usually have this effect on her. It was nothing her children were actually doing to her—it was what she was doing to herself by allowing the situation at work to bother her after work. As she calmed down, she could see how the situation at work had made her angry and that was actually upsetting her children and not the other way around. Unintentionally, she was blaming her children for how she was feeling. We are only human, and all of us have tendencies to become irrational, upset, angry, and bad tempered. And that's okay, as long as we can understand it for what it is—our problem, not our children's. By not blaming others and acknowledging how and why we are feeling a certain way, we can proactively do something to change those circumstances for the better.

However, when we think others are making us feel a certain way, we become powerless to change anything. It's as if it's out of our control. This can be an excuse not to take responsibility for our own lives or to abstain from responsibility of our children's behaviour. They are simply naughty and no matter how much we tell them, there's nothing we can do, leading to labelling our children as naughty and their behaviour as either good or bad.

But what exactly is good and bad behaviour?

REGRESSION OR REBELLION?

There will be times when children regress—that is, their behaviour or development seems to take a backward step, this is perfectly natural, especially when they are experiencing transitions like starting school or when they are ill. These are to be expected. By being proactive and finding the cause of their stress or frustration and helping to alleviate it, this usually resolves itself. However, rebellion can rear its head as part of becoming independent too. So, no need to panic if it's a rebellious phase they are going through. It's normal for children to resist routine and to flex their authority from time to time.

In fact, as a Mum, Child carer, and Therapist, I would be more concerned if they passively didn't.

A child who has their own mind is a good sign of a healthy, happy individual.

That's why as parents we don't want to eliminate that and why we need to understand what exactly is good or bad, naughty or nice behaviour?

Sometimes, children simply don't know or understand what they've done wrong, and telling them off only adds to their confusion.

That's why we need to take our focus off punishment and discipline and onto education and explanation instead. Explaining and teaching our children why they should or shouldn't do something works more effectively than telling them off. Explaining helps them to understand. And when they understand, they are less likely to repeat any unwanted behaviour in the future.

Let me share a personal example with you to illustrate this point and to help us understand what good or bad behaviour actually is.

THANKS A LOT, SON!

To help differentiate between the two, I will share a true story that happened to me. Some years ago, I attended a parent's evening for my then six-year-old son who had recently started in a new school.

As I excitedly sat down, eager to find out how he was getting on in his new school, his teacher greeted me with something all parents dread to be told. That day, he had misbehaved and received his first red card (a red card is what the children receive for being naughty, and they get punished by not being allowed to go out at playtime with the other children).

My first thought was 'Thanks a lot, son, of all the days to misbehave, you chose today, your parents' evening to do it. How embarrassing, now I feel like the teacher is telling me off too!'

My second thought was, 'what could he have possibly done wrong to get a red card?'

His Teacher then went on to explain that when she had told the class they were having 'Tambourine Time' my son's enthusiasm overtook him as he jumped up excitedly and proclaimed, 'Yes, my favourite!'

As she could see from my face, I was still waiting and anticipating what he'd done wrong. So, she went on to say how bad she now felt for telling him off and giving the card to him, but she needed to 'quash' his enthusiasm.

Too perplexed to say anything and somewhat relieved that his only conviction was being too enthusiastic over tambourine time, I decided not to say how I felt about the matter. But deep down, I could not understand why a teacher would want to quash a pupil's enthusiasm for a music lesson she was teaching?

But more than anything, I could not believe the difference between a child being labelled naughty (in my son's case with a red card to symbolize it) over something that I (as a Professional Childcare Provider and Mum) would deem a good quality—which is enthusiasm for learning.

This clearly illustrates the difference between what one person deems as naughty or unwanted behaviour; another person could consider acceptable, even admirable behaviour.

Clearly, with so much misunderstanding involved in the adult and child relationship, our children may not be aware or even believe that they are misbehaving until it is pointed out to them by either their parents or a teacher.

Then, even after being told they've been naughty, they still may not see themselves as misbehaving but just as being curious or having fun.

The confusion lies in the fact that good and bad behaviour is really only a matter of opinion. Really, there can be no bad behaviour unless it is being observed by someone who believes it to be bad behaviour. The problem with that is everyone has a different perspective on what is good or bad behaviour dependant on their own ideas, unique perceptions, moods, individual experiences, and beliefs.

Consider this:

If Your child is having a tantrum whilst they are completely alone and there is no one present, not even you, to witness it, are they still being naughty, or are there any other words that you could describe their behaviour instead? Such as frustrated, angry, afraid, sad, or confused?

LABELS STICK

Labels such as 'naughty' or 'stupid' can stick. And just like superglue, even when removed, can leave unwanted damage underneath.

Maybe you yourself got stuck with an unwanted label when you were at school?

After all, we are all just children who grew up!

I don't mind sharing with you that I got glued to a self-limiting belief given to me by a teacher when I was younger!

I won't name Mr. Jones because that would be cruel, and I don't like name calling. But a maths teacher I once had told my Dad at parent's evening when I was only eleven or twelve years young that I:

'Wouldn't go very far in life and wouldn't be able to achieve much because I was no good at maths.'

My Dad still reminds me of this comment to this day, and I'm now forty-two years old. Just goes to show how long a label can be attached to someone!

Thankfully, that bully of a teacher who used to humiliate me in front of the class and throw board rubbers at his pupils was wrong!

I have a couple of successful businesses now, and guess what?

I can afford an accountant and can also use a calculator to do my own accounts if I choose!

If somewhere along the way our children have been misunderstood and they are now suffering this 'naughty' label that's attached to them like super glue, we must start to peel it off them before too much damage is done.

We show others how to treat our children by how we treat them. If we tell other people our children are naughty, that's what other peoples' expectations of them will be too.

Our children are never naughty, but their behaviour can be difficult sometimes. That's not who they are though. How they act today is not an accurate reflection of who they will become in the future.

Any child shown the right kind of understanding, patience, love, support, and guidance can be just as good as any other child. Behaviour, whether good or bad, is an in the moment reaction. Unacceptable behaviour only continues if it's misunderstood or not caught early enough, allowing it to become a habit. We can change our children's behaviour simply by changing how we view them. Stripping them of unhelpful labels such as 'cheeky' and 'naughty' and replacing them with more helpful ones such as 'good' and 'clever' or even 'curious'.

The more our children hear us and others, using positive words to describe them, the sooner they will start to believe them and act accordingly. And the sooner we will be able to effectively and positively manage their behaviour. We just need to change our perceptions.

SHIFTING PERCEPTIONS

It's not an easy thing to do, but shifting our perception is really quite simple. Let's demonstrate how easily we can shift our perception in an instant.

How Embarrassing!

Several years ago, whilst dropping my children off to primary school, one Mum angrily commented, 'Look at the state of that Mum!' as she pointed out another Mum to me on the school yard who was dressed in pyjamas. 'How embarrassing for that little girl to be brought to school by her Mum dressed in pyjamas.' She went on, 'Look, she hasn't even bothered to get dressed or make any effort to do her own hair, let alone her daughter's. She is such a bad mother!'

What would you have thought, if you had seen this Mum dressed in pyjamas, dropping her child off to school, looking rather unkempt?

Have a think, then write down your answers, and we'll come back to this in a moment.

Of course, this Mum was entitled to her own opinion just the same way as the other Mum was entitled to do the school run in her pyjamas; both just had a different perspective on the situation.

BEHAVIOUR IS A MATTER OF PERCEPTION

You see, behaviour is just a matter of perception. It's not actually what our children are doing that makes us annoyed, stressed, or upset, it's what we are thinking about what they are doing and the judgements we are placing on that behaviour. Knowing this can help us as parents to better understand our children's behaviour. This is a better alternative than always trying to change the behaviour itself, as sometimes this can be impossible. But how we view their behaviour is something we can easily change when we try. This is not to say that we should overlook or defend every wrongdoing they do. We still must lovingly guide and support our children's behaviour. When they do things they shouldn't, they need to know, as this is how they learn how to behave appropriately. But it's how we go about letting them know that's important. In future, to help us alter our perceptions of our children's behaviour, we could try to pretend that everything our children does or says is just their way of learning how to behave.

None of it is to intentionally embarrass, annoy, frustrate, or upset us in any way. We are just giving them the freedom and privilege to learn how to behave.

That's when educating and explaining helps.

Anyone who has ever spent more than five minutes in the company of a three-year-old will know that their favourite question is 'Why?'

And do you know why?

Let me share another story that happened several years ago, which helped me to gain a clearer understanding on my definition of good and bad behaviour that will help us to answer that question.

PUDDLES OF TEARS

One day, I was saddened to drop off a tiny three-year-old boy (he really was tiny for his age) who I cared for back to his house after nursery school.

There stood his Mother on the door step in floods of tears as she greeted me apprehensively with, 'How's he been today?'

She was obviously anticipating the worst. I dutifully fed back the information his Teacher had asked me to pass on, that he'd had another 'bad day again' at nursery and had been answering the teachers back and being cheeky.

I personally thought, this young boy was a bright and inquisitive three-year-old. Neither naughty nor bad. Despite the fact that while we were at the park that day, he'd also answered me back a number of times. While walking home, I had told him not to jump in the muddy puddles to which he'd persisted in asking me:

'Why not?'

Not one to answer with 'That's why!'

I exhausted every answer to his constant question 'But why?' with answers such as:

'Because you will get wet.'

'Because you'll feel uncomfortable.'

'Because your Mum will be mad at you.'

'Because you'll dirty your uniform.'

'Because you may catch a cold.'

'Because I said so!'

Until eventually, I had to stop and ask myself:

'Why not let him jump in the muddy puddles?'

I soon found myself thinking: 'It won't harm anyone really. We can always dry off and change our clothes afterward. Anyway, we get wet when it rains and we don't always catch a cold. Besides, it looks like lots of fun, so why not?'

It then dawned on me that this small boy's constant probing for an answer to his question 'But why not?' wasn't cheeky back chat at all. It was his way of genuinely trying to find the answers to why he could not do it?

My reasons such as he would get wet, seemed obvious and silly to him. Of course, he would. That's why he wanted to do it, that was all part of the fun. My excuses defied his logic, and that was the reason that made him persist with his questioning.

And it was his ingenious questioning that led me to question the restraints that we put on ourselves and our children each and every day.

If no one questioned things, progress would never happen in life. Science would not exist, and we would all be conditioned to do what we were told, following others mindlessly, regardless if right or wrong or whether something makes sense or not.

It's the same for our children, if they don't question people or things in life, then they won't be able to find the answers and progress. That's the beauty of our young and innocent children—when we say 'You can't do that,' they ask, 'Why?'

Not necessarily because they are being rude, but because they know that what we are saying they cannot do, is possible. We unwittingly condition our children to accept our rational reasons as right, when actually, some of them are absurd.

If our children question or break the rules, this doesn't necessarily constitute bad or naughty behaviour, as in the muddy puddles example. Often, unwanted behaviour is misunderstood for being naughty, instead of being viewed as a child's naturally, inquisitive, playful nature. The danger is, if some children don't conform or toe the line like everyone else, then they are classed as naughty, instead of curious.

Sometimes, we create rules for our children that are not even our own rules. Often, they are generic rules that have been passed down from our parents, teachers, friends, or are deemed acceptable by society in general, and we don't even question them. But that doesn't always make them right. Just because something has always been a certain way doesn't mean that it should stay that way forever or that everyone has to follow the same rules as everyone else. We need to remember this when implementing our own rules for our children to follow. Before we tell our children that they cannot do or have something, we must first ask ourselves, why not?

Do our reasons really make sense to both ourselves, as well as our children?

BACK TO THE BAD MUM

Anyway, back to the dishevelled, disorganized, irresponsible Mum, who dropped her child to school dressed in pyjamas.

Or should that be... back to the loving, selfless Mum who had been bedridden for months and was very ill but wanted to take her daughter to school that day no matter what, as it could have been her last chance?

Back to that ill Mum who on that one day had mustered all her strength and effort to fulfil her child's wish of dropping her off to school again, maybe for the last time.

Looking at it from that perspective, how does that now make you feel?

From this new perspective, write down your thoughts and feelings now.

Did you think there was going to be a good explanation, as to why a Mother would wear pyjamas to school?

Or did you initially think the same way as the other Mum who presumed that she was a bad mother?

The first scenario ignites anger and frustration for the woman in pyjamas but the second evokes sadness and loving empathy for her. Yet, it's the same woman being observed doing the same thing, the only thing that's different is how the person observing perceives it. Everything is not always what it seems. Which is why we shouldn't be so quick to judge others or their behaviour based on our own perceived thoughts and emotions.

Our children's behaviour may be perplexing to us at times, but it's not all bad. Sometimes, it's just misunderstood. There's always a flip side to every label, even the good ones!

I'll prove this to you later on in the book, when we look at our children's so called positive and negative traits and we examine the perfect child in a little more detail.

CONSCIOUS PARENTING

When we shift our perspective and try looking at how we react and respond, instead of trying to control, change, or stop our children's behaviour, we become more human again and less robotic in our parenting approach.

Just like a robot is run by a computer, our subconscious mind also runs our daily actions and reactions that way based on programmed habits from the past. These habits can be useful coping mechanisms and can free us up to deal with other things, such as emergencies or new, unknown experiences. Our subconscious mind helps us out with day to day tasks, making us able to multitask. Such as enabling us to spot a free parking space on a busy road whilst navigating rush hour traffic with a car full of kids listening to the wheels on the bus for the zillionth time. This essential part of our subconscious mind keeps us safe and sane at the same time. It's a positive auto pilot mode that lets our mind successfully filter out the distractions going on around us. Allowing us to drive automatically without thinking about each step such as mirror, signal, manoeuvre. But when it comes to relationships, it's staying conscious that counts. People and circumstances change, but habits don't, unless we make a conscious effort to change them. When we are not conscious of our own behaviours or try multi-tasking our children with other things, over time, we lessen our ability to connect meaningfully with them.

AUTO PILOT ADVANTAGE

Auto pilot parenting can have its advantages for our children at times too. When I was originally writing this chapter, my then young daughter cleverly realised I was auto pilot parenting. Chatting away to me, she was tuned into the fact I was not actually listening to her properly and not engaged in the present moment with her. Unaware of this auto pilot parent mode, I was eagerly writing away when she casually asked me if she could have some chocolate. I replied 'Yes' without realising. It was not until she was excitedly unwrapping it saying, 'Yes, chocolate, yummy,' did I realise what I had agreed to. No big issue, it's only a bar of chocolate, maybe?

The problem is, as children grow up, they start to pick and choose their moments to ask for what they want. Cleverly choosing those moments when we are distracted and when they know we'll respond on auto pilot, i.e. agreeing to whatever as we are busily distracted with other things.

Advantageous to them, but detrimental to us if we end up agreeing to something without realising it that's a bit bigger than a bar of chocolate. Had I agreed to go and buy my daughter a new bike without realising it, then that would've been a big problem.

How could I have gotten out of that without upsetting my daughter?

I couldn't have said, 'Sorry but I wasn't really listening to what you were saying'. That's just as bad as going back on my word. But giving in to what I had unwittingly agreed to out of guilt, would have only exacerbated the situation further. It's better for us to become more aware of ourselves and to pay more attention to our children and what they are saying, instead of giving in or going back on our unconscious word. We can do this by becoming more aware of those moments when we are most vulnerable and changing our auto pilot ways.

AUTO PILOT ASSUMPTIONS

Vulnerable moments happen when we are busy or distracted. This creates an open invitation for miscommunication, misunderstandings, unwanted behaviour, and conflict. Not noticing what's going on around us or listening to what our children are saying makes us fall into the trap of making assumptions. When we make assumptions based on previous past experiences or on what we think is happening, there's a risk of being wrong.

Here's an example. While Auto Pilot Mummy is in the kitchen making lunch for Baby Johnny and Toddler Tommy, Baby Johnny starts screaming and crying in the living room. Immediately, Auto Pilot Mummy assumes that Toddler Tommy must have done something to hurt Baby Johnny because that's what he normally does. But as she was not physically present at the time of the alleged incident, she doesn't know for sure what happened.

At that present moment, she does not fully understand the situation, so she continues to tell Toddler Tommy off and react on Auto Pilot mode, assuming that Tommy must have been the cause of Baby Johnny's outburst. This results in a confused Tommy who now ends upset as well as he knows he wasn't the cause of Baby Johnny's crying. Tommy now decides that in future, he will do what is expected of him and hit his baby brother as he's getting the blame for it anyway. He then ends up being the cause of his Baby Brother's crying in the future to get him back for getting him into trouble when it wasn't his fault. All this drama leaves Auto Pilot Mummy stressed-out, fearing whenever she turns her back, Toddler Tommy's is going to hurt Baby Johnny. All the while, poor Baby Johnny who was only crying because he was so hungry still hasn't had his initial needs met. Now, due to all the commotion, his lunch has been delayed even further, leaving Mum, Tommy, and Johnny upset and a self-fulfilling prophecy established.

SELF FULFILLING PROPHECY

A self-fulfilling prophecy develops when parents and children try to predict how each other will behave and come to expect that behaviour in certain situations. These predictions are not always true, but directly or indirectly, they can become a reality. Our beliefs and expectations in them can actually encourage them to happen. We then end up automatically getting annoyed or transferring blame onto our children which eventually becomes a habit we no longer notice.

If we expect our children to react badly whenever we say they can't have or do something, then our expectation of conflict makes us more hostile and prepared for a fight. Children can pick up on this from our body language, stance, or tone of voice and end up conforming out of habit to what is expected of them. Then when told 'No,' they act as they feel they should by throwing a tantrum. If we continue to act on Auto Pilot mode and shout 'No!' We create a vicious circle of explosive reaction. This creates a volatile situation where no one can win. It's not that we want to tell our children off for the sake of it all the time. Neither do our children want to be deliberately naughty to upset us either. It just becomes the norm after a while, and we either don't notice ourselves reacting this way or we don't think there's anything wrong with it.

The main culprit to Auto Pilot Parenting is our perceived lack of time. This can mean a smacked bum or the threat of taking their favourite toy off them is a quicker solution to end conflict. Admittedly, explanations are time consuming, but they do save time and tears later on.

MISSING OUT ON THE GOOD TIMES

When we take the time to explain why certain behaviour is not acceptable, we have a chance to teach our children, and this way, their unwanted behaviour becomes a learning opportunity.

This not only proactively prevents these problems or behaviours from reoccurring in the future, but time together is more enjoyable.

Although, we can still fall victim to Auto Pilot Parenting tendencies when we're spending enjoyable, relaxing time with our children too. And it's important to become aware of these occasions. We want to spend time with our children, but are we really enjoying that time together or does it sometimes feel like a duty?

Most of us can remember a time rushing our children's bedtime story in order to get it over and done with only to realise when they asked a question relating to it that we didn't even know what the book was about. We were more than likely thinking about what we were going to cook for supper, or what we have to do tomorrow in work rather than wondering if Tiny Ted would ever find his dog again?

This is when what should be enjoyable 'quality time together' starts to become an everyday chore or inconvenience to be ticked off our to do list. We're usually tired, bored, or feeling like we should be doing something else more important such as replying to that back log of emails or attending to that pile of ironing. Although we may be present in body, we are somewhere else in mind. This means missing out on the parenting 'good times.' Unfortunately, the 'bad times' tend to demand our attention, but the good ones can easily go by unnoticed. Noticing those times when we're acting on Auto Pilot mode means we can stop and refocus our attention back onto enjoying time with our children and break the habit.

HOW WOULD WE COPE?

We can all remember that moment we brought our first-born home from hospital. I remember that snowy February day, my husband Paul putting the car seat down in the middle of the living room and us both staring at our new arrival for what felt like hours.

We were just in awe of her and scared and anxious at the same time.

All those fears surfaced.

How would we cope?

What do we do if she cries?

How will we know what she needs?

When?

And why?

What if we don't know how to be good parents?

Now, as I approach my daughter's sixteenth birthday, as a Mum, I feel so privileged and happy to have come this far. To have learnt so much. But more importantly—to feel lovable, loving, and loved. The pride and love I feel for my children every day are overwhelming. Making that difficult birth and all those doubts and fears pale into insignificance.

Yes, even the toddler tantrums and teenage angst has been worth every minute. So much so, I feel saddened that they are growing up, and I long for those baby days back.

Yes, children change your life in many ways but always for the better.

It may be hard to imagine now when you're in the thick of dirty nappies and sleepless nights, but it's in those ordinary moments together that one day you'll linger with your memories longing to go back. Those night feeds, school runs, class assembly's, duvet days, and trips to the dentist will become the best moments in our lives. Today, they are ordinary, everyday events. Tomorrow, they will be the most extraordinary, priceless, irreplaceable, nuggets of time in our lives. Time that all too often we take for granted because we are disillusioned that the work and worries that occupy our mind are the things that need our attention the most.

Yet, neither now nor in the future will anyone or anything ever bring us the joy, fulfilment, or happiness that our children do.

But what happens to that joy, fulfilment, and happiness being a parent once brought us?

Where has the joy gone when our toddler has wet the bed at 3am and is demanding we fetch them a drink because they are thirsty?

Where is that pride hiding when they whack our neighbour's child over the head with a stick?

Where is the fulfilment when we are scraping that homemade fish pie in the bin because they said it tastes 'Yuk?'

And where has the happiness disappeared to when they get bored on a well- planned family day out at the beach?

Well, the potential for those fun times together still exists. The problem is as auto pilot parents, we are used to noticing those things that we dislike or disapprove of in our children more often than the ones that we do.

To help us refocus and refresh our memories and rekindle the parenting joy, happiness, and fulfilment we know is hiding somewhere, the following 'Mood Mover and 'My Child's List of Positives' exercise will help in reminding us of all that's good about our children.

MOOD MOVER

Each time we find ourselves overreacting, we can stop and try to shift direction. Once upon a time, we were our children's number one fan, we adored everything they did. Even a poo on the potty was cause for celebration and hugs of proud appreciation, but as they grow, the focus changes, but is it our children who change, or is it us who change how we view our children?

Our children are just seeking our love and acceptance the way they once did. Birth to one years of age, we are usually loved up, in the honeymoon period of parenting, but as they start toddling and tantruming, this slowly changes. We don't stop adoring our children, but we start to notice more of those behaviours we dislike more than the ones that we do.

To move our mood back to the honeymoon period, we can refresh our memories by making a simple list of all that's good about our children. What we like, love, admire, and makes us laugh about their personality, physical attributes, and achievements as a whole. Do this for each child, so for example: Here's My Child Holly's List of Positives to get you started,

She is:

1. Funny
2. Independent
3. Emotionally Intelligent
4. Self-motivated
5. kind and considerate
6. A good swimmer
7. Beautiful
8. Confident & Out going
9. Empathetic, helpful and friendly.
10. Perceptive and intuitive

Now your turn.

MY CHILD'S LIST OF POSITIVES—EXERCISE

To do this exercise, set aside five minutes to write down what you like, admire, and approve of in your child.

Think of your entire child's qualities and achievements, listing as many as you can think of. Remember to include even the small, seemingly insignificant things. If you have more than one child, then do a separate list for each child with their names as the heading, for example:

My Child's [insert your child's name here _____] List of Positives.

MY CHILD'S LIST OF POSITIVES—EXERCISE

1.
2.
3.
4.
5.
6.
7.
8.
9.
10.

Keep this list somewhere you can see it daily, and each morning for the next thirty days re-read your list, adding to it each time you notice something new that you like about your child. This exercise of focusing and appreciating more of our children's positive qualities offers a more balanced view and a clearer perspective on their behaviour, making us less likely to focus on the negative. Keeping our love and appreciation for our children fresh in our mind daily replaces Auto Pilot tendencies with more present in the moment loving responses. That's exactly what we will embrace in the next chapter, Present Parenting.

ACCENTUATING THE POSITIVES

Tantrums and unwanted behaviour are hard to ignore, but desirable behaviour is easy to overlook. Looking for the positives in our children can help us remain positive when it comes to coaching good behaviour.

Now we have a list of positives, those things we admire and like in our children, lets focus more now on the behaviour we notice than what they are generally good at.

Accentuating their positives instead of noticing the bad, again, will help us in this next exercise.

- One day this week, today preferably, focus only on your children's behaviour and attributes that you like, and write them down.
- Then, praise them whenever you notice their good behaviour. It's important to praise their efforts, not just their successes. By giving them praise and openly showing them appreciation and approval, this will not only make them feel good, but we'll feel good too.
- Notice how well they start behaving when you are being supportive, and when you are in a good mood.
- Talk openly to others in front of your children about how well they have done or behaved. Unless we want to give the impression to others that our children are troublesome, then we should avoid moaning or complaining about them to others or publicly challenging our children.
- Affirm to yourself throughout the day: 'It's easy for me to be a good parent because I have such a good child/children.' Even if it feels like a fib and you don't believe it at first, say it any way and see what happens.

Now, keep your lists in a place where you can see them often (if you go out to work, take them along with you in your hand bag, this way, your children may be out of sight, but they won't be out of mind). Add to these lists daily each time you notice something new.

Each morning when you first wake, and each night before you close your eyes to sleep, for the next thirty days, re-read your lists. You'll be amazed at the difference this small exercise can make to your relationship with your child.

It will help you to appreciate more of your child's good qualities, and while you focus more on them, you will be less likely to focus on their negative ones.

This gives you a more balanced and clearer view of your child and their behaviours whilst keeping that love for your child fresh in your mind.

You'll soon find yourself naturally replacing any auto pilot tendencies with more present, in the moment, loving responses.

When we have this love and clarity for our children as unique individuals, we are in a better position to understand their behaviour and see it for what it really is. This is what makes a perfect child appear where once we saw a problem, which is what we will uncover later on in this book. Let's first break this habit before we break the child.

BREAKING THE AUTO PILOT HABIT

When it comes to breaking Auto Pilot Parenting habits, all we need to do is:

1. Notice what we do or say.
2. Know why we do it.
3. Know when we do it.
4. Notice when we are about to do it.
5. Decide not to do it.

Keeping a journal of our thoughts and feelings can really help us to notice all the above. Writing down each time when we overreact to our children's behaviour, such as shouting at them, and including the circumstances that led up to that reaction will help us to understand not only our own reactions, but how our children felt (such as crying) as a result of how we behaved.

In the heat of the moment, it's hard to think clearly. On reflection, it's uncomfortable to see how that's made us behave and the impact that's had on our children. It's even harder when written down and read after some time has elapsed and we have cooled down. But knowing our motives and why we react as we do helps us to change. When we keep a journal of those times, we can look for any patterns forming. For example, do we get angry with our children first thing in the morning when we are in a rush to get to work, or last thing at night when we are tired and want to relax?

Armed with this knowledge of why and when we're likely to react on Auto Pilot, we can become more aware of when it's about to happen and notice ourselves getting to that boiling point before we erupt. This gives us time to stop ourselves and shift our focus, but to do this, we need to be more self- aware.

HOW TO BECOME MORE SELF-AWARE

Self-awareness and reflection allow us to respond to our children more appropriately. Although it gives us the opportunity to do something about our behaviour, it can be difficult to do.

Looking at our own behaviour feels more uncomfortable than dealing with our children's. Partly because we feel their behaviour is out of our control, but we have no excuse for our own. Fortunately, the more that we can practise looking at our own behaviour and seeing situations and ourselves as an outsider, the easier it becomes to reflect on ourselves and improve. Let's ease a little more of that discomfort now by trying the following self-observation, visualisation.

SELF OBSERVATION VISULISATION

- Close your eyes for a second now and remember a time when you recall overreacting to your child's behaviour.

- Observe your behaviour in this situation by imagining yourself as an outsider looking on, observe yourself from the sidelines as you see yourself responding to your child's behaviour.
- Visualise any physical reactions you have, hear those words you said, notice how you said them, including the tone of your voice and facial expressions. Feel those feelings that you felt as if they are happening right now.
- Now, see how your actions affected your child and notice how they responded to you as a result.

That time may be over and done with in the past, but this kind of reflective practise helps us to break any unhelpful behavioural patterns we notice emerging. Becoming more present and self-aware as a result allows us to identify our motives and influences how we treat our children in the future in similar circumstances.

Then, next time, we can honestly ask ourselves:

- Did we overreact?
- Did we cause or aggravate the situation?
- Could we have done or said something differently?

As our reactions up until now have mostly been unconscious (on auto pilot mode), then the more relevant question to ask ourselves now is, where did this learnt habitual way of responding come from?

COMPETITIVE PARENTING:

THE PERFECT PARENT TRAP

At one time or another, we all fall into the 'Perfect Parent Trap.'

Either competing with other parents or comparing our children with other children. Yet, despite how well our children behave, what they achieve, or how we perform as parents, this is never going to be a true measure of parenting success. Parenting Success can only ever be measured by how good we feel as parents and how happy our children generally are. We need to let go of our misconceptions of what a 'Perfect Parent' or 'Perfect Child' should sound, act, or look like.

We may secretly envy 'Perfect Pete' who post-gym always looks smart and sexy at the school gates, despite working all day and lunching with friends.

Or we may wish to be more like 'Super Stay at Home Sue' who gives up her weekends to bake cakes for the school fete, volunteering for everything and anything to help others out whilst being full time carer to her ailing parents, five kids, three dogs, and a husband.

In either case, people and circumstances are not always what they appear to be. Aspiring to be like any other parent will always make you feel far from perfect because you can only ever be perfectly you.

SUPERMAN VS WONDER WOMAN

Comparing yourself with 'Wonder Women' will not do wonders for your confidence. Nor will striving to be like 'Superman' make you really super!

It's this striving to be someone that we are not that affects our self-confidence and makes us overreact or submissively retreat and surrender to our children.

Anyway, 'Perfect Pete' and 'Stay at Home Sue' may not be as perfect as you think.

And you may not be as far from perfect as you may think either.

'Perfect Pete' may always look the part and work and play hard, but he may be lacking in other areas of his life.

Maybe he's an 'Auto Pilot Parent' who hasn't really got time to be 'Present' for his children because he's so busy taking care of his own needs.

And as for 'Super Stay at Home Sue', she probably has absolutely no time for herself or her own needs as she's too busy tending to the demands and needs of others. Making her secretly miserable and resentful.

Making neither 'Perfect Pete' or 'Stay at Home Sue' really all that perfect.

It's more likely their behaviours stem from an underlying need to prove themselves or to be liked and accepted by others than from them being a perfect parent to their children. In reality, one way or another, both of them will have a void in their lives their ego is trying to fill. And it's their egos that are insisting on painting this perfect picture to others as having or doing it all perfectly.

Don't worry though if you can identify with either 'Perfect Pete' or 'Stay at Home Sue' in yourself. One or both of them are part of all of us parents sometimes due to our inherent, competitive, parenting tendencies.

COMPETATIVE PARENTING TENDENCIES

Our competitive parenting tendencies arise because in order to fit in and be accepted by others, we feel under immense pressure to not only be perfect in every way but to also produce perfect children. Every aspect of our lives is affected by these competitive tendencies from our work to relationships. We have become so accustomed to improving on all that we do and becoming better than everyone else that no matter what we seem to do, it never seems quite good enough. And our children and our parenting are no exception to this perfection.

When our children are not performing well at school or behaving as we expect them to, we feel like we are failing as parents in some way, or somehow, our children are failing. As a consequence, we end up not only pushing ourselves to compete with other parents, but we also expect our children to compete with other children instead of allowing them to naturally be themselves.

This is not only time consuming, meaning less time relaxing and having fun with our children, but it's because of all this striving that as parents and children we feel like we are never arriving. None of us parents are perfect, and none of us will ever have the perfect child. Yet our ideas of perfection are usually the same as everyone else's. That is; perfect means conformity to other people's ideals, expectations, and standards. There is nothing wrong with trying to improve ourselves or helping our children to improve. But this improvement should not be measured against any other person. Instead, we should aim to help our children to improve on their personal best, and we should try to be better parents today than we were yesterday, not better than Pete or Sue.

As soon as we shift our focus from competing to self-improvement, it releases so much burden and pressure from not only ourselves, but from our children too. This is important because it seems that our children are constantly being compared and measured against other children from day one.

And that all adds up to a lot of competition in a lifetime!

Even before conception, we tend to make comparisons with other parents. We compare how long it took to get pregnant, how many hours we were in labour, to how big and how much the baby weighed at birth?

And these competitive comparisons are not restricted to just the positive experiences either. Even negative ones are cause for competition as we lament over who had the worst birthing experience or who's baby was hardest to try and breastfeed?

This later progresses onto our children's sleeping, eating, and toilet training habits, through to schoolwork, and out of school extracurricular activities.

It's pointless though, judging or comparing our children to other children in the milestone race. If our children are generally healthy, then they will eventually learn to crawl, walk, talk, and use the toilet independently.

They will get there in the end!

We just need to release the pressure we impose upon them to progress and have a little trust and faith in them.

We can relax in the knowledge that all children develop at different rates and are good at different things. One child may learn to walk at 9 months but still have trouble toilet training at four years of age.

And just because so and so's child can read at three doesn't mean they are going to be any cleverer or achieve more in life than your child who can't.

And what does it matter either way, anyway?

What would happen to our world if we were all qualified at the same jobs?

If all our children were Grade A students all wanting to become lawyers?

They would end up fighting it out in Court, literally, for the same jobs!

Who, then, would do the rest of the essential jobs that need to be done? The world would end up in a mess. Every parent and child has a place in life, where they are, to do what they do, for a perfectly good reason. Their presence is important, no matter who they are or what they do. This includes you and your child too!

CHAPTER 3:
PRESENT PARENTING

IF WE THOUGHT OVERCOMING auto pilot parenting and becoming more self-aware was difficult, then Present Parenting will help. Present Parenting is the opposite to Auto Pilot Parenting, which, as we've discovered, is an automatic response to our children where we physically see and hear them speaking but are unaware of what they are actually saying or doing.

Present Parenting is consciously parenting by staying present in the moment and being aware of everything going on around us. It's thinking before we respond, not just about what's going on, but how and why? It's understanding our children's behaviour and how they are feeling and taking all of this into consideration. Present parenting certainly makes our children's behaviour less of a mystery and parenting easier and far less stressful for everyone. Although, we can only experience this when we learn to lighten up and see things how they really are instead of catastrophising and making mountains out of mole hills.

Have you ever heard the saying, 'If you don't laugh, you'll cry?'

I know it can be hard at times. I had to fight back the tears when my two- year-old threw our brand new digital SLR Camera into a potty full of pee!

It would've been one of those perfect memory making moments to capture and look back on and laugh at years later now she's a teen. But at that time, the camera stopped working!

Our children's behaviour can be challenging, but is it really all that seriously bad?

Before we tackle difficulties and coaching our children's unwanted behaviour, we are going to have to learn how to stop taking everything too seriously and how to become more present.

LIGHTEN UP!

Lightening up is an important aspect of remaining present and having confidence in our parenting abilities. When we are too serious, little things annoy and frustrate us. We take every comment about our children or our parenting as a personal attack on us. This makes us defensive and reactive, causing us to lack confidence.

We won't win any prizes for being the most serious parent, but we will win the support of our children if we have fun with them. As well as the admiration of other parents who will feel inspired by our ability to relax and enjoy our children.

Seriousness won't work with our children, but responsibility will. And our children's happiness is our responsibility. Having a laugh and being calm and relaxed in the company of our children is what matters more than us looking like the perfect parent in front of others.

Who cares what other people such as our own parents or teachers think?

It's how we feel and how we make our children feel that counts. Laughing at poo and bum jokes may not be very mature, but who wants to get old anyway?

Not me, I want to be young and have fun as much as I can.

'Oh, my goodness, I've sent my child to school in odd socks! What will the teachers think?'

Who cares? Your child likes odd socks.

At least they are happy. The least we can do is be happy for them and stress less about the little things.

Whenever conflict arises between ourselves and our children, we can choose to let them be right, and we can choose to be happy instead. We don't have to get our point across. If it is not that important, we can choose to let it go.

Just because we are grownups doesn't mean we always have to be right. Telling our children off for every misdemeanour or feeling embarrassed by the shallow, judgemental opinions of others about our children's behaviour will not matter twenty years from now. But our children will remember and appreciate the rebellion in us that freed their spirit. More favourably so than the uptight, nervous wreck who tried to force them to be 'perfectly' not themselves.

We can free ourselves as parents by learning to take ourselves lightly. And accepting that the trials and tribulations along the way are all, funnily enough, just part of the parenting journey.

Our children have the best sense of humour, so let's laugh with them and at ourselves from time to time. We cannot be sad or stressed at the same time as being happy and relaxed. So, let's choose happiness instead and laugh our parenting cares and troubles away. This I know can be difficult to begin with, especially when you find your child's unwanted behaviour far from funny. This is what this book will specifically help you with, understanding your child's unwanted behaviour and accepting it, as well as your own.

It's easy to get sucked into a war without even realising it. When we are busy, as so often we are, we tend to run on auto pilot mode. We react to people and circumstances in the heat of the moment in a learnt way to help us cope with the many demands placed upon us as parents. But peace can be restored when we change the way we think and respond to our children's behaviour. But for this to work effectively, we have to become one team and remember that we're all on the same side.

ONE TEAM

Team work really does make the parenting dream work. My children's Primary School had the perfect motto: TEAM. Which stands for – Together Everyone Achieves More. You could feel the sense of that message resonating with staff and pupils.

When we feel part of a team, we feel like we are all in it together to help and support one another. It's important when Coaching our children's behaviour to bear in mind that we are on the same side. Working together makes you both stronger, happier, healthier, and more successful.

Parenting is not a battle of us against our children or vice versa. Neither should there be any competition between parents, there's no good cop, bad cop. It takes both parents, as well as any other carers who are involved in our children's life, to come together and agree on rules and routines.

If not, children become confused, angry, or upset, and eventually, they end up playing parents against each other. This tactic is the most common cause of parents arguing with one another. Therefore, we need to join and stand together as a team. We have to remain consistent, firm, and fair together. Making sure everyone who cares for our children does the same, sticking to the rules and routines that we have set and expect our children to follow.

This team effort approach ensures we are all on the same side, working toward the same goals. By creating one team, we will eventually get our children on side too, as they won't enjoy being alone against a team of many for long. Eventually, learning to get along with everyone and playing by the rules and routines will become their goal too.

A strong family or network support of friends and other carers, including childminders and teachers, will build a winning team together. Creating the foundations that will become our children's greatest support and security in life. Ensuring that no matter where they go or who they are with, they will have a safe base to turn to where they can rely on consistency, familiarity, and comfort.

That's why we have to develop that 'one team' mentality and why everyone who is in our children's lives need to be on the same page as us. Outside of the home, this can be difficult to monitor. It's more difficult to control outside influences, but we can't address our children's behaviour without looking at these and the impact they can have on our children, so we'll cover those in later chapters.

Our children, realising that everything we do is for their own sake—not for our own—and understanding that we're are not trying to spoil their fun but help them is key to getting them on side. This helps them to see that we have rules and routines for good reason, for their own happiness, health, and safety. Rules and routines help us to communicate with our children positively and effectively whilst they are learning how to connect and communicate appropriately with us and others.

LETTING GO AND GOING WITH THE FLOW

Letting Go of Control

Our aim as parents should not be to control our children, but to allow them the freedom to be themselves and to grow as unique individuals. Too much control can restrict our children's potential to become autonomous, decision making, happy, and healthy individuals. And the reality is, we can't control our children's every action or emotion even if we try. It's difficult enough trying to control our own actions and emotions, let alone our children's. That's why the only solution we really have is to release some of that control.

We can do this by acknowledging that our children's behaviour can be inappropriate and hard to manage or understand sometimes and accepting that's okay—we don't have to control it. If we persist in trying, we'll only end up frustrated and exhausted. This is when all the toil and struggle in parenting occurs. As soon as we learn to let go, we will feel a lot lighter, calmer, happier, and oddly enough, a lot more in control. Our children won't end up out of control if we cease to be controlling. As long as they have fair, reasonable rules and consistent routines in place, there is no need to worry. Rules and routines replace control with love and guidance and discipline for coaching. Creating less restraint and resistance. We can feel safe, then, to let go of some of that unnecessary control by trying out the following exercise.

LEARNING TO LET GO EXERCISE

- Today, choose fifteen minutes to spend with your child when it's safe to let go of control and relax. The only time you should intervene is if they are about to do something dangerous to themselves or others. As a proactive parent, your home environment should be a safe place to do this exercise but be more aware and vigilant outside.
- In that fifteen minutes, choose to let it be okay for you to let go of controlling the situation. If, for example, your child is painting or making a mess, pulling all their toys out everywhere, allow them to. It's okay for those fifteen minutes, you don't have to control anything.
- Really feel relaxed. If you are finding it difficult, remind yourself it's only fifteen minutes, and whatever it is your child is doing, it's not the end of the world. They are just having fun, and you're enjoying the freedom of not having to stop them or tell them off. You know that you can easily clean any mess up later on. If your child gets dirty, they can have a bath afterward, and washing machines were invented to clean dirty clothes. But for now, you don't need to worry about any of that. Yes, even the crayon on the wall or playdough on the floor. You can just RELAX!

This is your chance to let go for fifteen minutes. Relax and refrain from throwing fuel on their fire. Just step back and watch them and silently say to yourself 'It's okay' as you take in a few deep breathes and exhale slowly. Try not to breathe in and out too quickly or too shallow though, you don't want to end up hyperventilating. Over time, as we practice doing this exercise, we will soon realise that nothing catastrophic has happened. Then, gradually, we will master this art of feeling relaxed around our children, no matter what, even when we venture outside in public.

The more often you practice this exercise, the easier it will become. Even if they are throwing a tantrum in the supermarket, it's still okay. When they finish throwing a tantrum (and believe me, they will probably stop before the fifteen minutes are up, especially if we are staying relaxed and not reacting to them) then we can just carry on as normal and do our shopping as if nothing happened.

Of course, there will be occasions when we will need to exert some control over our children. For example, when they are young, it's necessary to insist they hold our hands when crossing the road. And this common sense approach never ends, even when we have teenagers. As a matter of safety, it's responsible of us to insist they be home at a reasonable time in the evenings. But there's a way in which we can do and say these things that's not controlling and that's without any tense and stressful emotions going on inside us. Such as gently taking their hand and explaining to them that it's only because we care about them that we're asking them to hold hands for their own safety, while pointing out the dangers of the roads and fast-moving traffic. This is far more effective than demanding that they hold our hand.

This way, we don't feel controlling, we feel loving. And our children don't feel controlled, they feel loved. Lovingly communicating what we want is the best way to start teaching our children how to behave. This method lasts a lifetime, other quick fix solutions seldom do. Smacking certainly becomes redundant when children turn to teens. We can't change how our children think or behave, no matter how much we try to control them. In fact, the more we try, the worse things become. But we can be a positive influence, and we do have the power to change how we think about their behaviour and how we respond. (Remember our shifting perceptions exercise with the Bad Mum earlier?)

But we can never make our children good by making them feel bad. That's why smacking, shouting, humiliating, and intimidating methods are ineffective.

What we'll likely find is that by explaining and talking things through and answering any questions our children have, that they do actually behave appropriately for their age most of the time. A lot of the time, children lack knowledge, experience, and understanding, so by us listening to them and filling in the gaps with explanations, we see their innocence more than insolence.

Children are childish. Tantrums at two are a normal, natural phase of development. Answering back at three, sulking at six, acting sly or selfish at seven and stropping and sleeping at sixteen can be too.

What we can do to help is try not to place too many unnecessary restrictions on our children or too much control. This only creates more resistance in them, and in ourselves too. Just like an elastic band, our children can end up stretching us to our limit. But we don't want to snap and fall apart, neither do we want our children to. They too are like elastic bands, and every time they are told what they must or must not do, the band stretches. The more we nag or tell them off, the further they stretch until—ping! The band snaps. They then refuse to accept our rules and routines, and they try anything and everything to oppose them. It's a fruitless task trying to control our children anyway, because whenever we ask them not to do or say something, they only go and say or do the very thing we told them not to.

Telling them not to ask for sweets when they go to Nanny's house is as good as saying to them, 'Ask for sweets at Nanny's house!'

Sweets is all they will be thinking about as they associate the two words 'Sweets' and 'Nanny's House'.

The 'not' gets lost in translation. In their mind, the pictures of sweets equals Nanny's House, and that is all that they can see. The more they try not to ask, the more they will want to ask. It's a lot like us going on a diet and not wanting to eat our favourite treats. Suddenly, the urge and temptation become stronger the more we try to stop or deny ourselves.

The best thing we can do is say nothing regarding the sweets and not give them the idea in the first place. But this is a form of letting go, which takes practice and trust. We want them to know how we expect them to behave of course, but the simplest way is to positively tell them and try turning negative statements into positive ones. (We'll go into this in greater detail, offering lots of examples for you to try out in Chapter 4 – The Art of Positive Effective Behaviour Coaching.) Until then, say nothing at all!

By learning to trust our children more, they become more trustworthy. They know that we expect them to be trustworthy, so they are. It's a responsibility that they become proud to have and hang onto. We just have to practice having a little more faith in them and going with the flow more.

THE SECRET TO STRESS-LESS PARENTING

Learning to trust our children and going with the flow starts with acceptance.

Yayyy, we finally discovered the secret to stress-less parenting... ACCEPTANCE!

When we can accept our children and ourselves, we start becoming who we authentically really are. We don't try to prove anything to anyone or try to be someone we are not. Then we are able to relax and feel a sense of inner peace and true confidence that's needed to positively coach our children.

Our children always know when we are acting and not being our real selves. They latch onto this and join in with the pretence. I've witnessed it a million times as a Childminder. I could be caring for children who are playing happily, acting as their sweet, innocent, sometimes mischievous selves, then along comes their parents to pick them up and BOOM!

They turn into a different child. They start playing up for their parents, either preventing them from having a conversation with me, crying, shouting, or doing something they know they are not supposed to be doing. They even smile while doing it, as if to say, 'What are you going to do to stop me now, mum?'

And mums are always graceful, as they say, 'Come on, little Johnny, don't do that please.' In a soft quiet voice that hides a roar of a lion and a promise that later when they get home, little Johnny is in big trouble!

But in that moment, parents feel powerless.

Acceptance is not feeling powerless and giving up. It's correcting their behaviour in a calm, confident, but firm and consistent way. No matter where we are, what we are doing, or who we are with. We never change our style, tone, or approach. This is not a promise that our children won't misbehave or still won't try to embarrass us in some way, because they will. But how we deal with it should still stay the same. This means we have to expect, accept, and be prepared to deal with it.

ACCEPTANCE

Accepting our part and knowing there will be occasions when the most diligent children will misbehave helps us overcome our auto pilot parenting tendencies. Only experienced Buddhist Zen's will ever truly find that elusive, inner peace and tranquillity that comes from living and practicing meditation alone. The rest of us, especially parents, will have to settle for fleeting moments of calm amid the chaos. Ups and downs are part of the parenting process, they don't last forever, all we can do is try to enjoy the rollercoaster ride while it lasts. Our children will grow up and fly the nest sooner than we think. And, guaranteed, the first thing we'll miss is the noise and chaos because it's their presence and energy that makes life complete and gives us a true purpose in life. Appreciating that and accepting the good with the bad behaviour will confidently set us apart from other parents and make us more conscious as parents.

If we can learn to let go of control and start to go with the flow more, even if only for a short while, we'll soon notice that it's not our children's behaviour that actually affects us. It's our personal interpretation of their behaviour that gives it meaning, along with our own emotions. Changing how we view our children's behaviour can help us to change how we react to them. Helping us to accept them for who they are, including their behaviour. As our children think and behave differently than we do, we can't project our own thoughts, feelings, and beliefs upon them then wonder why they don't act, think, or feel as we expect them to.

Young children think that the world revolves around them. At some level, they are right, their world does revolve around them. In their world, everything is 'Mine!'

But don't worry, they soon learn to understand, empathize, and see other people's perspectives, assuming that they don't have a condition that prevents them doing so such as autism, that is.

Until then, all they know is what they want. That's why they put themselves and their needs first, even if it's not what's best for them. It's their inbuilt survival mode and self-love that they are listening to. And we can't criticise them for that natural instinct.

As parents, we know what's best for our children, but we should still encourage them to have their own personalities and desires, even if sometimes they conflict with our own. When we do, they realise there's not just right or wrong answers or specific ways of seeing or doing things. Life is more complex than that, and different views, including their own, are important.

Children are extremely resilient, but they do need a little leeway to build on that resilience and learn by themselves through making their own mistakes. They can only do this if they know we are there to support them, no matter what, regardless if they win or lose or are right or wrong.

Allowing our children room to make mistakes and express their emotions is a token of our unconditional love. This is what will help them the most to grow and mature into capable, content, happy, healthy, and successful adults. Emotions build up, they don't just disappear because we tell them to, so we shouldn't ignore them or judge them or punish our children for having them.

We just need to relax and allow them to unfold and blossom. We can only do this by releasing unnecessary control. And by acknowledging how our children are feeling while still offering our love and guidance so our children don't use their emotions destructively or take them out on other people. When we do, we help our children to feel more relaxed and secure. As a result, their behaviour naturally becomes a lot calmer, and they feel a lot safer.

Think for a moment of the most, angriest, anxious, uptight, on edge person you have ever known.

Now try to recall how that person made you feel when in their company.

I bet you didn't feel relaxed and at ease.

You probably also felt anxious and on edge around them.

You can feel this negative energy. Like a contagious virus, it spreads to others.

Likewise, positive, calm, relaxed, and happy people spread those feel-good, healthy feelings too.

What kind of feelings are you sharing with your child, and how do you think they feel as a result?

For some insight, let's try the following 'Life as Your Child Exercise'

LIFE AS YOUR CHILD EXERCISE

- Close your eyes and imagine your child's shoes in your head. Now, see yourself stepping into them.
- Mentally picture yourself unable to go anywhere you choose unless instructed to do so by your parents, childminders or teachers.
- Now, see yourself having to go places you don't want to go or do things you don't want to do because a superior is telling you that you have to.
- Imagine having to learn things that have no interest to you?
- Then imagine having to eat and drink what you are told, when you are told to, not what you like, when you like.
- Imagine not being able to see people you want to, when you want to, such as friends? Also feel how it feels like being forced to visit those people you don't like?
- Now, picture yourself being made to go to sleep when you are not tired or kept awake when you are tired.
- Hear yourself being told off for things you simply don't understand or being told how you should or should not behave or feel.
- Now put it all together and see, hear, and feel, what it's like having your every move accounted for.
- How did spending time with your parents feel in this exercise?
- Now how do you think your child feels?

This exercise helps us to recognize how limiting life can feel for our children. It helps us to feel how feeling this powerless can be very frustrating. We know that we only have their best interests at heart, but they may not always see this.

It's important that we can recognize and be sensitive to our children's feelings. They lack not only freedom over their circumstances, but control over their emotions. Lacking control over their own circumstances and emotions exasperates their behaviour further, causing them to misbehave.

They are literally and figuratively fighting for their freedom to be themselves. If they lack some freedom to take safe risks and experiment in life, this can also have the opposite effect. Instead of hitting out with unacceptable behaviour, they can become immobilized and reserved. Children need a certain degree of freedom and responsibility in and over their own life. They need to be able to make choices and be free to make mistakes. This way, they learn to trust us as well as their own judgements.

Then they won't feel afraid to make the odd mistake or test the boundaries from time to time. This means that they will turn to us in times of trouble, knowing that they will get the support and assurance they need, instead of disapproval or punishment.

I know as parents (and probably the main reason why you are reading this book) our goal is to prevent or stop our children's unwanted or unacceptable behaviour.

Hopefully by now though, we can understand their behaviour is not all that bad.

When our children are proving hard to control, then it can be a soothing relief to know it's because they are healthy as opposed to just naughty. They are not naughty. All they need is some guidance, attention, or, sometimes, the opportunity to learn how to deal with a new situation.

When we find our children's behaviour hard, it's usually because we are trying too hard. We don't need to control them. We just need to learn how to go with the flow more and become more present. And there's no present like time and no time like the present to begin!

YOUR CHILD IS A GIFT ENJOY THE PRESENT

Our children are the present, they are a gift to us, and they are here with us now, at this present moment in time. That's why Present Parenting is the best gift that we can give to them, and it's the gift that keeps on giving. It's the gift of actively listening and devoting our time and attention in the present moment. But this requires effort, not because it's unnatural and we have to learn how to be more present, but because we've formed the habit of Auto Pilot Parenting, which is not natural but an unconscious coping mechanism in response to today's busy world. We just have to remember how to naturally be, which is what we will do through the exercises in this chapter.

Present parenting is really just a natural response or spontaneous act or exchange of love. At least it used to be when life wasn't full of so much business and distraction. Life has changed dramatically over the past few decades, meaning most of us today are forced to work and keep up with technology, and this has become a time consuming source of distraction, compared to the times when it was common for the mothers to stay at home while the fathers were the sole breadwinners. We are now having to consciously think about how, when, and with whom we are distributing our time and attention. We have to wonder sometimes how all of this change and advances in technology are affecting our children today?

Decades ago, children had a lot more freedom and fresh air. As I write this, the WIFI in my house has not been working over a school half term holiday, and both my teenagers are distraught. They can't play with their friends on their consoles online or chat on social media! 'Go out and meet your friends' I suggest, 'but it's raining' was their come back. It rained when I was a child but I was out in all weathers, embracing the elements, what's gone wrong?

What's happened to nature and being natural?

We can't and neither do we want to go backward in time, what we want is to be more present in this time. We all experience times when we are fully present with our children, when we're enjoying each other's company and can physically feel the exchange of love present. They are available to us daily, yet we're not revelling in those moments like we should. But when we are present, they are such powerful moments that they stay with us into the future. Such as the time when I was taking my son Dylan to the Dentist when he was little. We were crossing the road, holding hands, when out of the blue he said, 'I love you Mum'

To this day, I can still remember thinking how this was such a good moment in my life. I wanted to keep hold of it so we could experience that intense feeling of love forever. We were just going about our daily business, yet it was such an extraordinary, emotional moment for me, so much so that I can still feel those positive, loving, warm, fuzzy feelings deep inside me whenever I recall that moment. I'm not sure my son would remember it as significant, to him it was just an everyday thing. He simply told me how he felt at that moment. Had I not been writing this book at the time and had not written about it; would I have forgotten it too?

Who knows? But what I do know is we were both feeling the power of one another's presence. And as I did write it down, we can now look back upon that ordinary moment with fondness and appreciation of such a great time when we were both truly present together, enjoying one another's company.

As normal and mundane as a trip to the dentist with your child may sound, I can guarantee that in years to come, you too will realise how special those everyday moments in time really are, even if those moments don't feel like it today.

One day, those simple, everyday memories will be where you will linger longingly, wishing you could go back to. Noticing, appreciating, and being fully present in those moments we are spending with our children today is what Present Parenting is all about. Those moments, as said previously, really are some of the best moments in our lives, they're priceless, irreplaceable nuggets of time that all too often we take for granted because we are disillusioned by the concept that the work and worries that occupy our mind are the things that need our attention the most. Yet, neither now nor in the future, will anyone or anything ever bring us the joy, fulfilment, or happiness that our children do.

HOW TO PRACTICE BEING MORE PRESENT PARENTS

Present Parenting is not a tool or technique that we can learn how to use; it's a way of being that makes us mindful in each moment. None of us can learn how to become present with our children in the future, it's all about this moment we are now in. Otherwise, it wouldn't be called the present, it would be the future, or, unfortunately for some, the past.

Surely, we cannot be anywhere else but present in the moment that we are in, ... or can we?

Let's try a little 'Being More Present Experiment' now.

BEING MORE PRESENT EXPERIMENT

Choose a quiet time alone with no distractions when there's nothing you need to do, no where you need to go, and nothing you need to think about, and find a clock to watch. Looking at a clock will keep you focused on the present time.

- Now, for the next five minutes, do absolutely nothing but stand and stare at that clock and nothing else.
- Don't think about anything.
- Don't do anything.

I bet you didn't stay present in the moment, even though you were physically stood looking at the clock. I bet you were thinking of something other than nothing.

It's a good idea to write down any thoughts that you can remember from this five-minute experiment. That's if you actually stayed the whole five minutes and didn't get bored or distracted before the time was up.

As you try to write those fleeting thoughts down, you'll struggle to remember what they actually were. They were probably rapid, unnecessary images, feelings, words, or voices, now irrelevant and forgotten. A lot like they normally are when you are going about your day or spending time with your child. Imagine now your child is that clock and their time is ticking away. They are there now right in front of you, but if you get distracted by those other, less important things that bombard your mind intrusively when you are with your child, then that time will soon be gone! Our children are here in the present—forget to pay attention to them and they will soon be grown up and in the past. Leaving us with our thoughts and memories, of all those insignificant things that once seemed more important.

NO TIME TO STAND & STARE

If you grew impatient doing that experiment, then you probably felt you had no time to waste to just stand and stare.

If so, here's another one to practise that instead of wasting time, gives you the chance to do something you've always fancied doing but never had the time.

PRESENT PRACTISING ACTIVITY

- Think of an activity you would like to try out for this 'Present Practising Activity'. For me, cooking is a good activity to practise being 'Present'.
- Pick something stimulating or a bit challenging, this will keep you interested and focused on the task at hand for longer.
- Choose a time when you are by yourself to start with, it's easy to get distracted when our children are around.
- Now go and do it. If it's exercise, get up and go for a run, even if it's just up and down your stairs for five minutes. Try not to think of something that you'll have to wait to do such as taking up a new hobby like knitting. Of course, this would be a great present practising activity to do but not if you haven't got any wool or knitting needles as that'll become your excuse to put this exercise off until they arrive tomorrow. As we know, tomorrow never

comes. Whatever you choose, do it now. Not later or tomorrow, this is a Present Practising Activity—the time to do it is now.

- As you engage in this activity, stay focused on what you are doing and feeling in each moment. You may hear that annoying little voice in your head telling you, 'This is stupid, stop wasting time, you're too busy, there's lots of more important things you should be doing'. But don't let it bully you into unconsciousness. Stay present!

When cooking, I get absorbed in what I'm doing, I need to concentrate to prevent chopping a finger off or burning myself. I stay engaged by choosing to cook different dishes each time to challenge myself and keep me present, if I wander off mentally, I could ruin my evening meal, so I focus on the task at hand. This way, I experience the different tastes, textures, and smells, and I'm not thinking of anything else except what I'm doing, making it also therapeutic, as any worries are forgotten. Time seems to fly by in this flow state. Then once we practise feeling in the flow in new activities we enjoy, we know we can experience this day to day in general too.

If you can't think of a specific activity to practise being present in, and don't like cooking, then try practising while having a bath. Feel the warm water surround you, notice the sparkling bubbles floating on the surface and the scent of the soap. Feel your skin wet and soapy, and take in the full experience of having a bath. Luxuriate in this refreshing experience. How often do you bath without thinking about these things or without really enjoying the experience?

That's because when bathing, we are usually somewhere else in mind, and instead of relaxing in the present moment and enjoying the pleasurable experience, we take it for granted, and it becomes another Auto Pilot chore. Anything we do often tends to end up this way. We become desensitised by its familiarity.

FREE YOUR MIND

It's so easy for our minds to wander, robbing us of experiences in the present moment. They seem to have a voice of their own that just doesn't shut up at times, and it's that constant chatter that prevents us being present in the moment. We just have to learn how to distract it or temporarily turn it down.

Isn't it time to do those things we love for the sheer enjoyment of doing them? Freedom to indulge in our pleasures and be with those special people we love?

If not now, then when? When will you feel totally free to be in the moment and do nothing without feeling guilty?

If you only do one thing right now, then just let go of everything that's mentally cluttering up your head and watch the fog drift away. Don't worry, it'll be back tomorrow.

If you can free your mind of mental chatter, you'll free your muscles of tense matter. That means you'll relax. So, let's give it a go.

RELAXATION

- Switch off your electronic devices and all phones.
- Make sure no one will disturb you, and when it's safe to do so, either sit or lay down somewhere in a nice comfortable position. Surround yourself with cushions or soft warm blankets if that helps.
- Take in some slow, deep breathes.
- Feel where your tension resides and allow it to release as you breathe gently and slowly in and out. There's nowhere to go, nothing to do, and no one to see, so you are absolutely free. Free to let go and relax. This will be easier for some more than others. But don't worry about it, that will only restrict and tense you up some more.

- Just keep breathing, and as you do so, say to yourself:

'Let go.'

'Let go.'

'Let go.'

Don't just say the words, feel them.

- Practice this letting go and breathing to free your mind until you get bored.

I warn you, this state of pure relaxation and freedom of thought is addictive and hard to break, but it's a great habit to make.

CONSCIOUS COMMENTARY

Not one who can easily relax?

Don't worry, there is another way to stay present and drown out that mental madness called Conscious Commentary.

It's simply giving ourselves a running Commentary of everything we are doing. This helps to switch off our subconscious mind, the part of our mind that carries out Auto Pilot responses and mental chatter. For example, when preparing dinner, talk yourself through what you are doing, each and every step of the way:

1. I am now peeling the potatoes.
2. Let's cut the potatoes up and add them to the pan of water.
3. I'm setting the gas cooker to three.

It's not necessary to speak this Conscious Commentary out loud, although it will prevent your mind wandering off, and children find this highly amusing. You can, however, simply think each step in your mind. Even a simple activity such as peeling potatoes can conjure up memories of when you last ate potatoes... and, well... then you are no longer conscious of what you are now presently doing!

Start off with a three-minute period and then build up the amount of time you spend doing it over the course of a week until it adds up to one hour of training your mind to be present.

Daily rituals such as bathing or preparing dinner can be some of the most pleasurable parts of our day once we start appreciating them again.

We can all become present right now, this very second, by doing absolutely nothing. And can stay that way as long as we choose. Being a Present Parent is a conscious, in the moment choice that we always have. Just because we can all do it though, doesn't mean it's easy to do!

BUT WHY IS IT SO DIFFICULT?

As parents, we have other people dependent upon us, and with so many responsibilities and things to do, life is full of distractions. Mobile phones and computers which are supposed to help free up our time and make our lives easier end up doing the opposite, keeping us constantly occupied and in demand. Amid all of these distractions, when we work out the actual amount of time we enjoy daily with our children, present in the moment, it's more likely to be minutes not hours. Most children spend the majority of their time at childcare, school, doing extracurricular activities, in front of a screen, and sleeping the rest of the time. It's become acceptably common to rely on these new-age babysitters, and, sadly, our children think these are all normal. They've become hypnotized and habitually addicted to them. To the point where were we to take their digital preferences away in order to spend more time talking to us, it would feel more like a punishment to them, not a present. These all distract our children from our presence and prevent us from becoming Present Parents, adversely affecting our relationships with our children.

We know when our children are not really listening to us and are absorbed in a computer. Likewise, they know when we are not fully present in the moment with them. Understandably, reading that same picture book that has only four words in it for the hundredth time can be tedious, and not getting distracted by other thoughts or things can become an impossible task.

But when our children are young and still craving our attention, they know we're not mentally present, and this makes them feel as though they're not as important to us as they should be. Even if they are distracted themselves and uninterested in us on a conscious level—unconsciously, they will feel our vacancy, creating a void that keeps growing over time.

THINK MORE CHILD-LIKE

Children are naturally present in each and every moment. They see the world and are in awe of its beauty and newness, they're not tired of life. They enjoy exploring all it has to offer and have all the time in the world to stand and stare. The school run is a chance for them to appreciate the beautiful blue sky with white, fluffy clouds making unusual shapes. They muse at the sun shining on the dew drops, glistening as they dance on the lush green blades of grass. This beautiful love of life and nature is the reason why children wake up so early in the morning. They are excited about the adventure that lay ahead each day, and they don't want to miss out on anything or waste time sleeping. To children, the journey is as relevant as the destination. They couldn't care less about the pointless pot of gold at the end of the rainbow, they're more interested in the beautiful colours of the rainbow itself. If we can remember to think more like them again as we once did as children, this makes life a lot easier and more enjoyable, not only for our children but for us too.

We can practise this whenever our children wake us up early in the morning. Instead of getting annoyed, we could welcome their presence as the best wakeup alarm there is, reminding us that it's another fresh, new day, and that we are alive, well, and loved.

I know we're tired, busy, and don't have the time to waste standing and staring at trees and clouds. But do we have time not to?

Besides, the daily commute to work/school/shops or wherever else we need to go, it still takes a journey to get there, whether we stop to notice all the splendour around us or stress out about the traffic.

If only for today, let's try to think more childlike.

THINK MORE CHILDLIKE

- Wherever you are now, turn off the background noise and distractions around you such as TV, radio, phone, computer, or mental chatter of your mind.
- Then stop, look, and listen to nature and what is all around you.
- See what your child is seeing, hear what they hear, and try to feel how all that makes them feel?

It may sound a bit childish at first, but being more childlike is the core to being present. I recommend hypnosis, hypnotherapy, meditation, and guided meditations to most parents unless they have epilepsy or psychoses. It's not new age or weird in any way, it's just a form of slowing the mental activity of the mind down and fully relaxing. Something none of us are truly used to. We operate from the alert state of Beta. Most of us live on a daily basis with physical symptoms of stress such as tense, tight neck and shoulders, headaches, backache, and digestive problems such as IBS. We live with it because we think it's normal, we can't remember what it's like to feel totally at ease. Yet, feeling calm and relaxed is a normal state that is affected by how we are thinking in the moment. If our thoughts are focused on negative outcomes, our bodies respond to that imagined stress as real. As a hypnotherapist, I'm into different states of being. I love the Alpha, Delta and Theta brain wave states where I can access my imagination and manifestation potential.

For us adults, delta is a deep sleep state, it's a childlike state as children up to two years operate from a delta state, mostly from their sub conscious. Their brains operate at a low frequency of 0.5 to 4 cycles per second, this explains why babies sleep so much

Their conscious questioning mind is still to develop, and two to six-year-old children's brainwave states are 4 to 8 cycles per second and are known as theta, one of daydreaming, creativity, and imagination. That's why children under six take things so literally and believe everything you tell them. After six years, they tend to start questioning the tooth fairy. That's when they move into the alpha state, between 9 to 14 cycles per second, although, interestingly, alpha waves are present by the age of two.

Now their analytical mind starts to develop, and they start to draw from their previous learning. Eight years and over—they enter our adult, everyday state of 15 to 40 cycles per second, now they become conscious, logical thinkers!

For us grownups, these childlike states feel like a warm, calm, deep, sleepy, relaxing state of equilibrium, where we can change old programmed patterns of unhelpful, outdated behaviour and absorb learning effortlessly. Here, we have access to our creativity, and we are not critically analysing, although we are in an intense, focused state of concentration, and we're not actually sleeping. We all experience these different states naturally. When we sleep, we go from the alert, engaged, focused mind of beta, to alpha, to theta to delta, and that's then reversed as we wake.

We have to think of our children as walking around in these trance-like states, open and receptive to everything in the environment, soaking up, learning without any awareness they are doing so. They may not be paying conscious attention, but we as parents must!

PARENT WATCH: OBSERVATIONS

Another way that we can understand life from our child's perspective and learn a lot about them too, which can help us help them, is by watching them. When it comes to being present, they are our best teachers. Mindfully observing our children is an invaluable skill, and done regularly, it's a great proactive, parental tool that keeps us informed on their development and progress.

Presently observing is more than just watching our children and making mental notes. It requires using not only our eyesight but our intuition as what our eyes see is not always what our children feel.

Present Parenting requires us to:

- Watch with our eyes.
- Think with our head.
- Listen to what's 'not' said.

- Feel and parent from the heart.

That's the secret to Present Parenting.

PRESENT PARENT WATCH

Making notes on our children's behaviour to reflect on helps to spot problems and their cause and effect. The following pointers will also help.

- Once a week, for ten minutes, watch your child going about their business. Pick a time where you won't be in demand so your child can act as natural as possible without needing you.
- Note the time as well as what's happening, this will offer clues as to why they behaved a certain way. Say we observe them at bedtime brushing their teeth, they may appear to be misbehaving when possibly they're just tired?
- Act inconspicuously so they don't become suspicious or notice you watching them. Children act differently when being watched. You will get the most natural observations if you pretend to be doing something else.
- Don't intervene in what they are doing or engage in conversation with them.
- Notice their body language, tone of voice, and how and when those change. By being aware of these, it's easier to spot any unwanted potential behaviour in the future and distract or change them. You will also be able to notice when they're behaving constructively and reward them for doing so.
- Write down what you observe, being as independent as possible.

These notes are not only good to reflect back on, but you may notice things that surprise you. Maybe your child can become frustrated easily or are good at concentrating and persevering on certain tasks.

PRESENT ACTIVE LISTENING

We won't always understand our children by just observing them though; Present Parenting involves actively listening too. This is not only what our children want from us more than anything else, but if we want them to listen to us, we must first learn to listen to them. When we actively listen, they know they have our undivided attention, and they feel listened to, respected, and valued. It's more than just being present and getting the gist of the conversation. It's deep listening where we hear more from the silent pauses and unsaid than from the key, surface words that we normally hear in everyday conversation. It's where we hear the voice of intuition, and that's the most advanced form of Present Parenting.

It's using our ears, heart, and head to understand what our children are really saying. Heeding every word while being able to let go of any judgement, personal opinions, beliefs, or thoughts of what we are going to do or say next.

We can be too 'present' at times and talk too much, and this is when we miss so much vital information. We need to stop whatever else we are doing and look our children in the eyes and show them they have our undivided attention as we listen carefully to what they have to say. We learn more by being available whenever our children want to talk than we do from questioning them when we want answers. It's challenging for children to wait until we are ready, as they easily forget what they were going to say. This may not always be convenient—but asking them to wait results in them vying for our time and attention, so listening when they want to speak can save time in the long run.

PRACTISING ACTIVE LISTENING EXERCISE

Active listening is a skill worth practising because it's the proof that we are present in the moment. So, let's practice the following exercise.

- Let your child know you would like to spend some time having a chat about anything they wish. Doing this in advance gives them a chance to consider what they would like to talk about, helping them feel valued and important.

- Choose a quiet time to chat when you both have plenty of time without distractions.
- As you listen, you may feel the urge to guide the conversation, comment, or add your opinions or advice, but refrain from doing so. They may want to discuss something that's troubling them but may not want your opinion or a solution. Allow them to find their own answers to their problems first.
- When they ask a question, answer them, but aim to listen for more than ninety percent of the time. When you do ask questions, avoid closed questions where they can only answer 'yes' or 'no.' Ask open questions instead, ones that start with 'What?' 'When?' and 'Why?'
- Nod, smile, and pat them gently if it's appropriate, this will confirm that you are really listening and empathizing with them.
- Observe their body language to find clues as to what they are not saying.

LOSING TRACK

They'll probably want to discuss a made-up scenario that happened to one of their toys. Undoubtedly, you will find yourself distracted or bored mid conversation. This is normal and helpful when practising and improving your Present Active Listening skills. Just notice your own distracting thoughts and let them go. Then bring your attention back to your child and what they are saying. Avoid admitting you weren't listening, instead, say, 'Sorry could you say that again, I'm not quite sure I understood that last bit?' This way, they'll feel we are trying to clarify something and we're taking the time to really listen and understand what they are saying as opposed to getting bored of their conversation.

MIND YOUR P'S & Q'S

As well as listening to what our children are saying, it's vital we become more present of what we are saying. Words are very powerful weapons or tools depending on how they are used. Minding our P's and Q's and encouraging our children to keep their own self talk positive is crucial to their self-esteem and well-being. That little voice inside their head can be their worst critic, telling them that they can't, shouldn't, and that they are not good enough. It's their interpretation of what they think others think or feel about them, but it's not always true. They tend to believe and trust significant people in their life—Father Christmas and the Tooth Fairy are two untruths that they believe because we told them so.

As young, impressionable children under seven years of age, everything we say to them resides in their subconscious mind. They haven't the faculty to reason, judge, or question what we say reliably, so they just accept everything.

Their main opponent in life will be their own voice inside their head. Being mindful of our own words ensures we don't add to their negative self-talk in any way. Innocently, we may utter 'No one will want to be your friend if you don't share' but it's not true that no one will want to be their friend. If they hear us saying this before they've even learnt the concept of sharing, then they could carry those beliefs with them forever. As adults, they may come to believe that the reason they have no friends is because they are too selfish and don't like sharing. Acting out this self-limiting belief could end up sabotaging every relationship, creating a self-fulfilling prophecy where they ignore or reject anything to the contrary of this. Regardless if negative comments are casually said in the heat of the moment or they're sandwiched between a hundred compliments, a single criticism can last longer than a million compliments.

We covered how labels stick previously, but it's worth reiterating how children labelled naughty or stupid over time start believing and acting that way because they think it's expected of them. This produces feelings of inadequacy, worthlessness, guilt, or anger. At challenging times, they will hear that voice in their head saying, 'You're stupid' and 'Don't even bother trying' unless, we make a point of teaching them that mistakes are not stupid—they are learning opportunities that build confidence in their ability to cope with anything. They need to get into the habit of convincing themselves that they 'Can do' as opposed to they 'Can't'. Quotes such as 'Winners never quit and quitters never win' and 'I can't is just 'I can with a T for Try' and Virgil's' 'They are able who think they are able' along with affirmations, condition and convince our children that they can succeed. We'll look into this further in chapter 9.

NO TIME LIKE THE PRESENT

So, now we know there's no time like the present, and no present like time!

If you knew this was your last day ever with your child, you would hang onto their every word and not waste a single second. One day will be the last day you spend together, so make the most of now and start to live in and enjoy each and every moment from now on. Tomorrow is promised to no one, stay present and be generous with that time because our time and influence in our children's lives count. We are the ones who teach them how to listen to others by how we listen to them. We are their most influential role models, as we'll see in chapter 8—Powerful Parents, and we have the power to end the battle and win the war, as we will uncover next.

CHAPTER 4:
END THE BATTLE AND
WIN THE WAR

'WHY DO YOU throw rocks before you, the path ahead is smooth?' A wise Sage once said, he must have been describing parenthood.

OLD HABITS DIE HARD

When children are proving hard to control, the easy path often seems... well... too easy!

So, we dismiss it as an option and carry on the hard way out of habit.

But as already said, when we find our children's behaviour hard, it's usually because we are trying too hard.

What if there was an easier way to control their behaviour without being a controlling parent?

SCHOOL HOLIDAY DESPAIR

One long summer school holiday (you know, the ones that seem to go on forever—or you soon will!) A Mum came to see me in despair saying she had lost control of her children and didn't know how to get it back.

She felt as though she was (in her own words):

'Fighting against them in a constant battle about everything and feeling defeated all the time.'

My advice, which surprised her, was to go along with her children whenever she felt totally powerless and to see what happened.

I wasn't suggesting she leave her children to their own devices and let them walk all over her, encouraging them to take advantage of her apathy. I just wanted her to accept and allow their demands temporarily while she regained her confident composure and sense of authority and self.

This was to show her children she was not accepting their behaviour powerlessly. Instead, she was showing them that she didn't mind either way how they behaved.

This reverse psychological approach not only confused her children somewhat, but as intended, it equipped her to deal with their behaviour.

PEACE AT LAST

There was no more struggle.

Instead of feeling powerless and beaten, she was able to manage normally challenging situations easily.

By her thinking that she was choosing how to feel, she felt empowered rather than feeling powerless. Feeling powerless suggests there isn't a choice how to act or feel and nothing one can do. The truth is, there's always a choice, and parents are never powerless. We have all the power, all the time.

I assured her that her children would soon get fed up of misbehaving once they realised she did not care, and they weren't getting any attention for their behaviour. What she soon noticed was her children had stopped wanting or asking for the things that previously she was not allowing them. By her not disallowing her children the things they wanted, the battle was over.

They hadn't won the war though because, really, they didn't want those things they were fighting for in the first place. All they were interested in was the battle. So, she ended up peacefully winning the war.

Going with the flow means allowing peace and acceptance. We may not associate the two with parenting. But they are utmost when it comes to moulding desirable behaviour in our children.

Whatever our children do or don't do, we can still feel at peace in ourselves.

As long as we accept our children and their behaviour as a normal part of growing up, then occasionally, when we want them to do as we say, we will feel free to let them have their own way.

IF YOU WANT THEM TO DO AS YOU SAY LET THEM HAVE THEIR OWN WAY!

Sometimes, if we want our children to do as we say, then we have to let them have their own way. This may sound contradictory to having rules in the first place!

But if we are constantly on our children's case for every minor thing, we all end up miserable and worn out, making us ineffective.

This is not to say that we must always let our children have their own way or allow them to flout the main rules. The rules are the rules, and they must follow them at all times.

Occasionally, it's fine to let them get their own way with regards to other less important behaviour though that doesn't have a fixed rule in place.

If we allow them some responsibility and freedom in less important matters, then they are likely to take the important rules more seriously and to understand the give and take principle better.

The bizarre thing is, when we do allow our children their own way, usually, they end up doing things our way anyway!

MY LITTLE WELSH GIRL

When my daughter was young, she had a Traditional Welsh Girl outfit. It had a lovely black bonnet with a white ribbon that she loved. She loved it so much so that she kept nagging me to let her wear it to bed at night.

Of course, this would end up in a huge argument as I tried to convince her to take it off and put her pyjama's on!

Then, one night, after much debate, I decided to use a little reverse psychology and agreed to let her wear it to bed.

After about ten minutes, she came running out of her bedroom, asking me to take it off her and put her pyjamas on as it was so itchy and uncomfortable.

Job done, I'd given in and won!

When we allow our children to make their own choices, they lack resistance. And when given the option, they usually choose not to do the things they thought they originally wanted to do.

They must feel free to make the choice though. It's important that they feel that we have no resistance or strong preference what they do either way. They then realize they no longer need to fight against us as there is nothing to fight about.

When there's no resistance, everyone wins.

But if we always say 'No' or get confrontational, our children will persist, and inevitably someone will lose.

Choosing our battles wisely enables us to identify the times when it's okay to let them have their own way.

CHOOSE YOUR BATTLES WISELY

Our children have a reason behind how they behave. They just can't always articulate or understand it. That's why it's best to choose our battles wisely.

If we follow the footprints in the snow, we'll usually find the Gruffalo, but often discover there's a different story at play.

We need to get a clear perspective of the situation first by staying Present and Proactive. This will help us to find out the reasons behind our children's behaviour rather than focusing on the behaviour itself.

Then when we discover the source of their behaviour, we'll know how best to coach them in another direction or when not to get involved.

SEVERING THE UMBILICAL CORD

Everyone is an individual in their own right.

We all enter and exit the world alone (even twins come out separately).

Yet, it's easy to forget that our children do not belong to us and that they are separate people from us.

They have their own preferences and personalities that are unique to them as individuals.

Also, they don't perceive the same problems as we do. Therefore, they have different expectations of themselves and their behaviour than we have. But we often feel how they behave reflects on us as parents.

Sometimes it's not just what others expect from us as parents or what we expect from our children but more about managing our own expectations

We need to be willing to let go of that invisible umbilical cord that we feel still attaches us to our children to be able to feel the freedom and separateness that exists between us.

If we could only feel this freedom and change how we perceived our children's behaviour, then our own negative emotional state would change.

Then, whenever our children did something that we didn't like or agree with, we would be in a better position to deal with it.

That's often easier said than done though. Not only do babies and young children get separation anxiety, but lots of us parents get it too. That's why loosening the reins can be challenging for most parents.

It means releasing control, and this can be frightening.

As parents, we worry that if we don't control our children, then they will become out of control and go off the rails. But no one ever wins in a battle for control.

None of us were born to be controlled. Babies and toddlers instinctively know this truth, that's why they cry, scream, and tantrum!

We are all free spirits, and from birth, we know this.

Children strongly fight any attempt at being controlled. They know it goes against their natural rights as an individual.

Often, we only try to control our children because we are afraid of what others will say, think, or feel about us. And this fear is what causes us to overreact.

CONFIDENCE CONQUERS

It's easy to overreact to unwanted behaviour, I want to write love conquers all (because I do believe that to be true, except when dealing with young children who often can't be reasoned with!), but young children simply don't have the capacity to rationalise and no matter how much they love us, it's their will that will take over. That's why love alone won't help us to manage our children's unwanted behaviour.

Then then the key is CONFIDENCE!

Overreacting and losing control of ourselves doesn't make us look, act, or feel confident to either ourselves or in front of others or our children.

It's ironically usually those 'others' who are causing us to overreact to our children's behaviour in the first place.

We then further complicate an issue by overreacting through embarrassment.

Our children will often embarrass us, so the best way to keep our composure is to expect it as normal.

Children often hit other children, say embarrassing things, and grass their parents up when they tell a fib. They actively love looking for ways to humiliate us in public—that is what they do—whether intentionally or unintentionally.

If we learn to walk our talk, that shouldn't bother us too much as there shouldn't be too many fibs or ways in which they will be able to humiliate us.

However, if they do find a way, it's not what they do or say that should concern us, but how we react to it and deal with them as a result. So, let's keep confidently cool.

More often than not, we will be more concerned with how others view us as parents and how they see us managing our children's behaviour than our children's behaviour itself.

Therefore, it's best to choose our battles wisely, but this takes a lot of confidence in our own parenting ability.

Knowing when to overlook certain unwanted behaviour in our children and knowing when to step in at other times is an art.

Don't worry, you can learn how to hone that over time.

That's why it's always best to know our own boundaries and to set rules and routines that our children are familiar with regarding behaviour. They need to know what we expect of them.

When we all know the rules, everyone will know how to act or react.

Let's take a typical scenario as an example, let's say you and your child are out with your friend and their child. Your friend's child and your child are running around playing, screaming, and shouting when you notice your friend doesn't seem to like the children being so boisterous and loud.

You then see them tell their child off as your child carries on playing regardless. Now, however, your child no longer seems to you like they are playing and having fun. Now they seem to be influencing your friend's child to carry on screaming and shouting, making you feel compelled to step in and tell your child off and to stop your child playing through fear of your friend judging you or your child's behaviour. You do this even though deep down you believe that your child is not misbehaving, just letting off a little steam.

This lack of confidence in your own parenting abilities or beliefs about behaviour then causes your child to become confused as to why you are telling them off and trying so desperately to stop them having a good time?

If they are normally able to play this way, they will be thinking; 'What have I done wrong?'

You cannot, of course, explain to them in front of your friend that your friend doesn't like their behaviour. Neither can you accuse them of misbehaving if you or your child do not believe that they are misbehaving.

On the other hand, say you stick to your integrity of firm, fair, consistent rules and allow your child to carry on playing. You will then worry that your friend will think that you let your child get away with misbehaving while feeling anxious that your child is influencing her child to misbehave.

Although, it's actually the opposite and is more to do with your friend influencing you with her rules which are different in comparison with your own.

Of course, we are assuming that the conditions are suitable for your child to be behaving this way.

For instance, it's okay for young children to run around screaming and shouting in the park but not at the cinema. We have to take other people and circumstances into consideration, but when we become confident in our own beliefs and rules, our own common sense will be able to guide us.

There's no one right way to manage behaviour, every parent and child is unique. There's no need following, copying, criticizing, or listening to other people's well-meaning opinions. We have to trust ourselves and believe we are doing the best that we possibly can for our children, and then we will find the right solutions.

Children misbehave for all sorts of reasons, and their reactions are automatic in most cases. They simply cannot regulate themselves as their prefrontal cortex, part of the frontal lobe of the brain associated with reasoning, concentration, planning, decision making, impulse control, risk assessment, delayed gratification, emotion, and logic, isn't developed enough. This can take years to mature, although most executive functions are developed during the teens, in some cases, this can take longer, stretching into the mid-twenties, sometimes thirties. That may be why some of us parents are irrational at times and become reactive instead of proactive. Until this point of development, children are using their emotional brain.

This emotional brain means usually when they appear to be misbehaving, they are just over excited, confused, scared, or unsure how to behave. They need to have confidence in us as their parents that we will correct them for the right reasons. By demonstrating self-confidence as a parent, our children will feel more safe and secure, and along with rules and routines, they will learn how to behave appropriately.

THE ART OF INTERVENTION

Knowing when to intervene in our children's behaviour and when not to is a fine art to master. It takes a lot of thought, patience, and practice. We have to stop ourselves from flying off the handle at every incident and decide if it's really such a big issue.

Does their behaviour warrant a reaction from us that is likely to upset not only our children, but ourselves too?

If it's not that important, then we have to learn how to let it go. Nine times out of ten, none of it's really that serious anyway. This is not an excuse to get out of correcting our children's unacceptable behaviour though—they have to abide by the rules in order to keep themselves safe and healthy.

It's knowing the difference between those times when we need to correct them and knowing when they have to learn how to correct themselves. For example, when they are squabbling with friends or siblings, it's not always necessary or helpful for us to jump right in and intervene.

It's important to step back and let them get on with it at times and let them argue amongst themselves and learn how to resolve their own issues.

This is the only way they'll learn how to get on with other people and how to resolve conflicts in a safe, nurturing environment.

When our children hurt the ones they love, it teaches them when they have overstepped the mark. It offers them the opportunity to apologise and make up, or forgive the other person too if they feel they were justified. Silly little squabbles can be resolved between children without adult interference, so if it's not our battle, then we don't need to fight.

FOLLOW YOUR OWN RULES

We can set the rules, but it doesn't always mean that our children will follow them. But we should follow them, because when we do, we increase the chances of them following them.

We should always endeavour to follow our own rules. If we have a rule about not wearing shoes upstairs, then we must follow that rule at all times, especially when our children are around.

If for some reason, we do happen to break the rules, then we need to be open and honest with our children by saying so, such as:

'Oh, silly Mummy, I just wore my shoes upstairs. I was desperate to get to the toilet, but I know I shouldn't do that because it makes the carpet on the stairs dirty.'

Here, they can hear us acknowledging we've done something wrong and why it is wrong to do it. But if we disregard the rule ourselves and then lie about it or try to cover it up, they will see that we do not take our own rules seriously. Then they will wonder why they should.

As powerfully influential parents, there shouldn't be one rule for our children and another for us.

A rule is a rule and that's the rule.

BE CONSISTENT, BUT NOT RIGID

We need rules, but keeping the balance right and not being rigid and unrealistic is essential. Children do grow out of some rules, and as time goes on, new rules will be needed. It's best to regularly check if our current rules still apply to our children and review and amend any ones that need changing, then be consistent and stick to them.

Our children will always push the boundaries if they know they can. They want to see how far they can go, and they are always checking if the boundaries are still in place. This actually makes them feel secure because having no rules or boundaries is frightening for a child.

They will not keep pushing the same boundaries if they know we are being fair and consistent because they will realise it's just wasted time and energy trying. But they have to know what those boundaries and rules are to begin with.

That's why we can't crack under pressure by giving in or allowing boundaries or rules to be moved or broken. We need to mean what we say and stick to it consistently.

'No' means 'No' not 'Maybe.'

CHAPTER 5:
THE 5 GOLDEN RULES

MAKING THE RULES

RULES AND ROUTINES ARE our potent arsenal to Coaching our children's behaviour positively and effectively. They are also the cornerstone of all happy, healthy, and successful children.

All good coaches and players play by the rules. Yes, we want our children to have their own mind, be assertive, and use initiative. We want them to also be creative and not to feel confined by too many rigid, unnecessary rules. Yet rules and routines give safety and structure to their lives. In today's chaotic, busy, overloaded world, it's important to have them to prevent our children becoming overwhelmed and lost in the sea of choice.

Rules and routines form the foundations for good behaviour while ensuring that corrections are given lovingly, fairly, firmly, and consistently. If not given this way, then we end up giving discipline or punishments out of frustration, despair, apathy, or anger.

This way is ineffective in managing unwanted behaviour as the message and purpose of correction and what we are trying to teach our children is lost.

This type of discipline only serves to end up reinforcing unwanted behaviour instead of preventing it.

We don't want to ever punish our children. We only want to correct their behaviour. Explaining and teaching our children right from wrong in order to prevent the behaviour reoccurring in the future, is best.

If, however, they do not listen to us or they persist in flouting the rules with inappropriate behaviour, then we have to correct them in a non-intimidating, non-physical way. A way that they understand which is age and stage appropriate.

Children need to know the rules.

They learn from being told their boundaries and what is expected of them and when they are crossing the line just as much as they do from freedom to be themselves. Freedom to be themselves doesn't mean we let them behave inappropriately. Our children feel secure and safest when we are in the parenting role and we can manage them appropriately. This way, they know exactly what it is that we expect of them.

When we set rules, we don't need to control our children. They learn to control their own behaviour just by following the rules.

DON'T HAVE TOO MANY RULES OR RESTRICTIONS

It's best to clearly define the rules upfront, keeping them realistic and easy for everyone to follow and understand. Ideally, when deciding on the rules for our children to follow, we only want a few really good rules, not loads of pointless ones.

We can make up rules for everything and anything, but with so many to keep track of, they soon lose effect after a while and get easily forgotten.

We need to be sensible and choose ones that are really important to us.

The thing about rules is, everybody will have different ones that they feel are important, and that's okay.

As long as we are clear on our own rules and don't have too many that are easy to forget, then our children will know which ones to follow.

Rules are important to us as parents because we will only know if our children step out of line when both ourselves and our children know where that line lays in the first place.

We can't assume that our children always know right from wrong or can read our minds and know that we disapprove of something. We need to tell them what we don't want them to do but we must then be clear on how we want them to behave instead also.

Telling them off is not enough. In most cases, they will just do the same thing again.

We have to lovingly explain what they have done wrong and why.

This can be difficult if they've upset or embarrassed us, but we have to learn to set our own emotions aside.

We may think that they should have known better, but obviously, they didn't. Their brains are just not capable, because If they did know better, they wouldn't have done it in the first place. Most pre-school children are honest to a fault, ask them outright did you break that ornament or eat that cake or hit the dog, and in most cases, they'll openly admit it was them. They can't lie because that's a skill they learn as they get older and understand consequences. Once they realise we can't read their minds and we don't really have eyes in the back of our heads, then the fun begins, and those tall stories can get quite interesting.

They think and act in the now and go for instant satisfaction, that's why they appear selfish and me, me, me, orientated.

I'm not trying to justify their immature behaviour, but a lot of the time, they need compassion not condemnation. Once we can understand why they act as they do and how that can be out of their control, then we are in a better position to help them develop those areas of learning.

The first time, we can grant them the benefit of the doubt, but repeated unacceptable behaviour after we have explained what we want and expect from them in future means they have misbehaved intentionally.

This is where rules become a great measure of misbehaviour, because if they know the rules beforehand and they deliberately go against them, then they are clearly misbehaving.

When they do this, we can lovingly explain the error of their ways, but sometimes, it's necessary to give them consequences.

However, we cannot have rules for everything. So, our children will in the absence of rules inevitably step out of line from time to time. This is our opportunity to point them in the right direction and get them back on track. Telling them off when they were unaware they were misbehaving only confuses them. It's this confusion that causes them to get angry or upset and to misbehave further.

All our children ever want is to understand the reasons behind things.

Such as why we have the rules we have.

And why we expect them to behave a certain way.

As already said, each of us will have our own set of rules based on our own beliefs, morals, and lifestyle preferences. You need to personally decide those for yourself. But all rules should cover five foundational key aspects.

I call these the Five Foundational Golden Rules to making the rules.

Before we set the rules that we want our children to follow, there are the five things our children need to know when it comes to the rules that we need to clearly communicate to them—which are as follows.

THE 5 THINGS OUR CHILDREN NEED TO KNOW WHEN IT COMES TO THE RULES ARE:

1. The Specific Rules. What we want them to do or not to do beforehand, i.e. be in bed by seven pm.

2. That there is a good reason for those specific rules we expect them to follow and for how we expect them to behave in certain situations. i.e. They need their sleep to enjoy playing with their friends at nursery in the morning.

3. That we mean what we say, and we will do what we say we will do as a consequence of their actions. This means we will carry out corrections when they do not follow those rules. Such as, if they don't go to bed on time tonight, they will go to bed earlier tomorrow night.

4. That they have been told and have had fair warning what they can expect as a consequence of their behaviour, and have been given the chance to correct their own behaviour before we give them corrections.

5. That the rules are fair, and we love them and only have their best interests at heart.

If we make these five golden rules clear to begin with when creating rules for our children, they cannot fail us in managing our children's behaviour. Let's elaborate on each one now.

1.   WHAT WE WANT THEM TO DO OR NOT TO DO—THE RULES.

The first point is about communicating to our children in advance the rules we want them to follow i.e. what it is exactly we want or don't want them to do. Sometimes we have to state what we don't want, as there's no alternative. Such as, no eating or drinking in the car, there's no better way to state that rule. However, as explored previously in our negatives to positive statements, where we can, we are better off stating how we want our children to behave rather than telling them how we don't want them to behave, i.e. 'Keep your drink in the cup' as opposed to 'Don't spill your drink!'

There's no point telling our children off after an incident if we haven't been clear enough in establishing the rules of conduct beforehand.

Establishing new rules is not an easy or instant task, but it's important that we do implement some in our children's life. We can insist that they follow our rules by being consistent in what we expect and persistent in implementing them.

DON'T MAKE UP THE RULES AS YOU GO ALONG

What we can't do is make up the rules as we go along. Our children need to know them in advance, and we need to be clear on what it is we expect of them ourselves.

It can be very frustrating for our children if one day we allow them to do something but not the next.

If we want them to trust us and follow our rules, then we need to take our time setting a few good clear rules that don't change easily, often, or for no reason.

Making rules up as we go along is far worse than having no rules at all. Our children will never know where the boundaries lay or what is expected of them from one day to the next if we do.

This is a very confusing and scary situation for a child to be in and could result in them thinking that they are naughty.

Especially if we tell them that they shouldn't have done something that they didn't think at the time they weren't supposed to do.

They may quite innocently have been totally unaware that what they were doing or saying was wrong. And this can be upsetting for them to discover.

Allow me to share another true story with you that my son encountered when he was younger.

At primary school one day, he was asked by his Headteacher what he was doing.

He was, in fact, hiding from his friend in the school corridor as a game of hide and seek. But when he honestly answered, 'I'm hiding from Joe,' the Headteacher reprimanded him, saying that he was speaking to her like something she had stood in on her shoe.

This really confused and upset my Son. So much so, he came home and told me all about the incident in tears. Had he really been trying to be rude to the Headteacher, I doubt he would have reacted the way he did or told me about it.

I also knew that it was not in his nature to be rude, especially not to a Headteacher whom he respected. He was just honestly answering her question without realising that he could be coming across as rude or arrogant.

From the mouth of babes, and in his own words, he told me innocently:

'I was confused and felt bad that I had done something wrong. But I didn't mean to. It's just she doesn't know me like you do, Mum, so she didn't understand me.'

I'm not sure if she was annoyed at my son for hiding in the corridor or the way in which he honestly answered her question?

Either way, my son did not know the rules.

2. THAT THERE IS GOOD REASON FOR THOSE RULES OR HOW WE EXPECT THEM TO BEHAVE

If our children understand our reasons for wanting them to behave a certain way, then they are more likely to cooperate with us.

Rather than just telling them what to do, such as, 'Put your coat on now!'

It's more effective explaining to them why it's important to wear their coat when they go out in the cold.

They have to understand why they must do something and not just because it's naughty not too.

Naughty is just a word, and children can't understand what that word feels like.

They can, however, understand if we give them examples that they can relate to. For instance, if they have hit another child, we could try reminding them of the time that Susie pushed them off their tricycle and they banged their head. Reminding them how it hurt so much they cried and that's how little James is feeling now they've hit him on the head with that wooden block.

This may prompt them to apologise or feel some compassion toward the child they have hurt or at least feel some remorse for what they have done.

This way, in time, our children will come to realise that we do have good reasons for our rules and how we expect them to behave. And also— that our rules are not optional. Having taken the time to make the rules, we need to make sure our children follow them.

The easiest way to do this is to ensure rules are:

- Firm
- Fair
- Consistent

- Compulsory

As powerful, confident parents, we don't nag or plead with our children to follow the rules.

We have good reasons for them, so we simply need to state clearly that:

'This is the way it is, and it is this way because_____' then fill in the blank with our reasons which are, Firm, Fair, Consistent, and Compulsory.

3.   THAT WE MEAN WHAT WE SAY, AND WE WILL DO WHAT WE SAY WE WILL DO

This lets our children know in no uncertain terms that we mean what we say and we will do what we say we will do. Carrying out corrections when they do not follow our rules as a consequence of *their* actions.

This means staying strong and sticking to our rules and not giving in or giving up just because the going gets tough.

All children are demanding, and when the going gets tough for us, then that's exactly when our children get going, so we have to be prepared.

They will most definitely rebel and complain about the rules in the beginning. This is when we will need to summon immense, inner, physical and mental strength. But guaranteed, our children will come to like the security that those rules bring if we stick to them. Then we can enjoy the easier life that comes from clear rules.

All of us at some time can relate to saying one thing to our children but after some persistent nagging from them we end up giving in and doing the opposite. But having inconsistent rules is just as bad as having none.

Inconsistency signals to our children that boundaries can and should be moved, and rules are there to be broken.

Hence, the battle begins. We think they are not playing fair, and they think we are not fair. We must stick to our guns and be prepared because our children will push those boundaries. Not because they're naughty though, but because we have let them.

EMPTY INTENTIONS

Just as bad are empty threats that we have no intention of keeping.

We shouldn't say to our children as a punishment that they're not going to their friend's party when we've already bought the present, RSVP'D the parents, and we know deep down we're going to take them anyway.

When we do this, we lose all of our parental powers, respect, and any chance we may have had of getting our children to take us seriously.

As a result, they have all the power back in their hands. They know now our rules and threats aren't real, they can be easily bent and broken. Storing this empty threat for future reference is what inspires them the next time they decide to do something wrong.

EMPTY PROMISES

Empty promises are just as bad as empty threats.

As empty threats tend to reinforce unwanted behaviour, we need to reinforce good behaviour patterns by praising the behaviour we desire in our children when we see it. As well as carrying out any promises that we've made our children for good behaviour.

When we have promised our children that we'll take them to the park for behaving well at the supermarket, then we need to make sure we do take them to the park. If we don't, we will unwittingly be encouraging them to misbehave next time we go shopping.

Keeping our promises keeps our children motivated to please us.

However, every time we give in to our children such as taking them to the party when we said we wouldn't because they had misbehaved, we reinforce that behaviour which we do not desire.

Our actions need to correspond with our words.

'You wait' or 'That's it, now you are in big trouble!' Are not clear consequences for our children's actions.

They are just clichés that we say in the heat of the moment when we don't know what to do or say and when we don't know how we are going to manage our children's behaviour.

In short, it's parenting on Auto Pilot mode!

We should also refrain from the popular warning, 'Wait until your Dad/Mum gets home!'

If we want our children to listen to us, then we have to be the one to confidently correct any unwanted behaviour immediately.

Telling our children off for something that happened hours ago is not fair or effective. A couple of hours later, they would have already forgotten all about it and won't understand why we are telling them off now.

In their mind, they've probably been good since then, so it's in the past, gone and forgotten.

So, let's keep promises and keep 'Present'.

BE FIRM

We have to be firm. This means not making threats we cannot or do not want to carry out. No party means no party, no matter what. Never mind they are expecting our child, or we've bought the card/present/new party outfit for them, or we've made plans to do something while they are at the party.

No reason should ever be enough to go back on our word when it comes to correcting our children's behaviour.

This is how we teach our children that for every action, there is indeed a reaction and consequence.

4.   THAT THEY HAVE HAD FAIR WARNING
We are playing fair when:
   • We make sure in advance that our children understand the consequences of their actions if they decide to break the rules.

- When we give them plenty of warning and a chance to correct their behaviour.

If they decide to carry on breaking the rules or pushing the boundaries of what is acceptable, then we have to show them the consequences by carrying out any corrections that we said we would.

Warnings ensure our children understand what we expect of them and are vital in giving them the chance to correct their behaviour.

These warnings and instructions on how we want our children to behave help us as much as our children. They can proactively prevent any confrontations developing. As long as we always warn our children in advance of the consequences of their actions if they break the rules. Warnings such as counting one, two, three, are popular and can work very well, but our children need to know there will be a consequence to their actions at the end if they do not listen.

So, no: One, one and a half, two, two and a half, two and three quarters, nearly three, then at the end—nothing.

Then if they fail to take us up on our warning, one more final warning of the repercussions is all that's needed: e.g. 'If you do not stop screaming at me now, then as I've already warned you, we will not go to the park.'

Then, if they still proceed and ignore us, we tell them that we are not taking them to the park because they would not stop screaming. While reminding them that we gave them the chance to stop, but they carried on. Then we leave it at that.

We don't get into an argument with them, it's no longer open for negotiation or discussion.

Although, if they persist in screaming, we can calmly ask them if there's anything else they would like to trade for being able to scream?

Maybe they would prefer to scream than watch TV?

Maybe they would like to trade being able to scream for their usual bedtime story later?

But as a bargaining tool, we never bribe them with treats that they wouldn't normally have e.g. 'If you stop screaming, I'll give you a biscuit.' This is an extremely slippery, yet convenient slope to fall down. One we can rarely get back up from.

Once we start bargaining unwanted behaviour for treats, we lose our ability to correct behaviour positively or effectively, and again, they are in charge.

Every time they fancy a biscuit, they will have learnt to misbehave in order to get what they want, then we find ourselves rewarding bad behaviour.

The trade for misbehaviour is only for trading the privileges that they are ordinarily accustomed to. However, a word of caution here, if we keep taking away their privileges and they are left with no toys or treats, then something is not working. Either the warning has not being given adequately, or they have just succumbed to giving up all their privileges and have become accustomed to it.

This is not a satisfactory or effective outcome for anyone. Soon, they'll become angry and resentful at us for taking what is theirs. They may even surrender to their unwanted behaviour, giving up on being good completely, feeling hopeless and demotivated.

Again, the behaviour becomes a perpetuating, self-fulfilling prophecy. Our children come to believe that is how they behave and the consequences are always to lose something.

Then the behaviour never gets corrected or resolved.

The aim should be they want to please us or behave appropriately and to keep hold of their privileges. Then everyone's happy.

We never want to intentionally punish, hurt, or deprive our children of anything, no matter how naughty we perceive them to be. We just want to help guide them in the right direction.

When we have firm, fair, consistent rules in place, then our children will already be aware of how we expect them to behave and gradually need less and less warnings as time goes on.

Nonetheless, we always need to let them know before we enter a new situation, how we want or expect them to behave. Then it's up to us to step in with a warning if they don't behave accordingly. We should never ignore the opportunity to correct our children's inappropriate behaviour. We are coaching them for their own sake.

And when they correct their own behaviour, we must remember to praise them and point out the good that has come from it, e.g. 'Thank you for not screaming anymore, now we can both go to the park and have fun instead of staying in the house miserable.'

If we notice and express to our children how pleased we are with them, whenever they correct their own behaviour, we encourage them to behave in the future. They will then feel that the rules are fair and that we love them.

5.   THAT THE RULES ARE FAIR AND WE LOVE THEM

Part of being fair when it comes to rules is paying attention to how our children are feeling. It's easy to get carried away with the rules and not notice how they are affecting our children.

Rules should be used to help us parents, as well as our children, have clear guidelines. We don't want to act like the boss. We want to be our children's guide and teacher. Someone who listens to and values their opinions and is there to show them how to behave appropriately.

For this to work, we have to be willing to see things from their side and talk it through. If a rule seems unreasonable to them, we should be willing to adapt it too if necessary. This does not mean getting rid of the rule but maybe altering it slightly if needs be.

It's about being fair to everyone. Sometimes, rules need changing as our children age. For example, seven pm may have been a reasonable bedtime when they were six, but not at sixteen.

Whatever age or stage our children are at, we always need to make it clear that when they misbehave, it's their behaviour we sometimes dislike, not them.

When they scream abuse or say they hate us, it may seem tempting to join in. Getting them back because they have hurt us may feel justified, but is it fair to act like the childish behaviour we are trying to change?

We simply have to kill them with kindness, as they say, and let them know that we love them and only have their best interests at heart.

LET THEM KNOW WE LOVE THEM AND ONLY HAVE THEIR BEST INTERESTS AT HEART

We set rules out of love for our children because we have their best interests at heart. And we should let them know this is why.

Once they get this, they will learn to listen and trust us, modifying their own behaviour over time.

Our children may understand it's wrong to hit another child and they should apologise.

They may also know they should wear a coat out in cold wet weather.

If, however, they don't want or choose to do those things, then that's generally because they don't understand what we are asking them to do is because we love them.

There can be no war where love is concerned, and when love is the central motivation.

Children only rebel if they feel like we are out to spoil their fun or upset them. When we explain we want them to wear their coat so they don't get wet and catch a cold because that could mean they'll miss their friend's party on Saturday, they learn to reason and do what's best for themselves and others.

This way, they are more likely to selfishly conform to our wishes. There is no other way, really. If we allow them not to wear their coat out in the cold wind and rain and let our children do as they want so we don't upset them, they lose. They are the ones who suffer as a consequence. If we make them wear their coat, we all lose, they feel unhappy, and we feel bad for upsetting them.

Children are self-centred. If we can use this to our advantage and convince them that our rules and routines are to benefit them (which incidentally they are anyway) then we're more likely to get them on side, and everyone's a winner!

We may not always feel we have the time to justify everything we ask our children to do, but we don't really have the time not to.

It's quicker to explain to them that we only have their best interests at heart than it is to get involved in an argument with them.

Arguments and bad feelings only end up demonstrating the opposite of what we are trying to convey, which is that we love our children and only have good intentions.

Now we are all clear on the rules, it's time to make the perfect child!

CHAPTER 6:
HOW TO MAKE THE
PERFECT CHILD

WELL, YOU'VE ALREADY MADE them perfect. They are perfectly themselves, even though their behaviour may sometimes seem far from perfect.

The perfect child is only a matter of perception though, which is not always true.

And not all of our children's imperfections are really that bad, it's just a matter of how and who is judging them.

This can be a great comfort to most parents, helping us to relax a little and accept our children for who they are instead of trying to control them or their behaviour.

If we view our children's opinionated personality as 'undesirable behaviour' but view another child's 'conscientiousness' as good behaviour, then with these judgements, it can be difficult to approve of our children's behaviour.

But no behaviour is good or bad, unless we think it is. As we've realised, what one teacher or parent views as negative [naughty], another may see as positive [nice].

Of course, we want our children to be nice and enthusiastic, but too keen can mean they are regarded as loud and boisterous.

We may also want them to be persistent when learning or pursuing tasks, but if they persist in nagging relentlessly for something they want, then they can quickly become annoying.

In our attempts to mould good children, we can sometimes unknowingly send them mixed messages of what is a good or bad quality within them.

This can inhibit their natural characteristics or abilities if we do not realise our error and allow them the freedom to be themselves.

And it's okay to let them because it's often those characteristics that we disapprove of in our children that are actually the very attributes that the majority of us admire most in grownups.

THE PERFECTLY IMPERFECT CHILD

We regard these good or bad traits as positive aspects in adults, but despite this, these same very traits can appear negative in our children.

Yet it's our children's imperfect traits that actually help to make our children perfect. So, let's look at their traits and how their imperfections are actually perfect.

Read on to discover a brief description of the most common 'Good and Bad' traits and why certain traits such as persistence can be helpful to our children. And how other qualities that appear desirable, such as conscientiousness, can actually have a negative effect on them.

As we go through the following fourteen traits, choose one word out of each pair that best describes your child.

PERFECTLY GOOD AND BAD TRAITS

1. CONSCIENTIOUS OR INFLEXIBLE?
2. PERSISTANT OR NAG?
3. CONFIDENT OR ARROGANT?
4. ASSERTIVE OR BOSSY?
5. ENTHUSIASTIC OR HYPERACTIVE?
6. HUMOUROUS OR CLASS CLOWN?
7. OPINIONATED OR INTOLERANT?

CONSCIENTIOUSNESS OR INFLEXIBLE?

If our children are conscientious and they always comply and follow the rules obediently, then we will no doubt have a perfectionist in the making. However, perfectionism is not as desirable as we may think. Our children may feel confined to those rules and life can become pretty rigid for them.

This can be frustrating, especially if they find themselves in a situation that requires some 'thinking out of the box' and creativity. Following precise rules in life may cut off their resourcefulness. They may believe that there is only one right way to do something and get anxious or stressed if things aren't as they expect or to their standards, making them upset and impatient with not only themselves but with others who don't do things right.

If they are always doing as they are told and always following other people's rules, this could hinder the development of their own ability to make independent decisions or judgements. Then, when eventually they are confronted with having to make their own decisions, with a lack of direction or rules, they will find it difficult to think for themselves.

This will cause them to doubt themselves, and instead of doing what they want or need, they will be constantly seeking other people's approval in every new thing that they do.

Not only will they suffer from self-doubt, but their self-esteem will become dependent on doing things perfectly right in order to please others. This inflexible way of thinking will actually make our children more judgemental of others, especially those people who think differently to them or who break the rules. Being conscientious not only restricts our children in their creativity and approach to tasks, but it has the added disadvantage of taking them longer than others to do things and complete tasks. This can be especially difficult as their conscientious nature may burden them with more than they can actually handle or deal with.

If, however, we are perfectionists as parents and impose perfectionism onto our children, this can actually have the opposite effect. We could make our children unconscientious as they withdraw from any challenges or cease to try in order to avoid the pitfall of feeling 'less than perfect' or 'not good enough.'

Worse still, they could rebel against us and our unrealistically high expectations and rigid rules. This rebellion is not always so bad though, some of the most successful people in life are non-conformers who do things their way, and they get good results.

PERSISTANT OR NAG?

Our children not listening to us and their relentless nagging is a big part of unwanted behaviour. Still, it is this trait known as persistence that our children will need to succeed in life.

If they gave up as soon as we said 'No!' then they would not have really tried.

Every successful person in life, no matter what field they are in, require persistence. When it comes to overcoming objections and persistence (a pre- requisite of most jobs, especially for sales people, leaders, and politician's), then we should take lessons from our children.

By listening and observing them in action, we can see how our children are the best teachers in perseverance. It's not always that they want to nag us for the sake of annoying us. Often, they just want something and can't get what they want any other way.

They don't have free will like we do. If they want to go somewhere or have food or drink, they have to rely on their skills of negotiation to get what they want.

No matter how tortuous their tactics, we have to admit that winners never quit and quitters, well... never win.

Do we want successful children or those who give up easily?

CONFIDENT OR ARROGANT?

There is no such thing as an overconfident child.

Confidence is not something our children are born with; it is something that they acquire. Therefore, a confident child has accomplished the right to be who they are.

Everyone wants to be more confident. One of the biggest entertainment producers today is loved worldwide, not for his physical looks or warm, kind personality, but for his unshakable confidence and self-belief.

Confidence is attractive and desirable. Everybody wants to be on the team who has the most confident leader. What we parents fear most is arrogance, but there is a difference between confidence and arrogance.

Arrogant people think they know everything and feel superior to everyone else, confident people know that they are not always right, but believe and trust in themselves, and they are not afraid to fail or admit when they are wrong.

We want our children to have the confidence to be who they are, not someone who always conforms like a personality-less robot.

We need to help them to build on the confidence that they already have while accepting their mistakes along the way.

We are in a digital, technological era where learning mental arithmetic in order to get a job in accounts, is no longer essential, and predictive text now writes for us. Now we have calculators and computers with software to do all that. Our children will have to stand out from the crowd, especially in job interviews in different ways. Getting a teen to look up from their mobile device to have a conversation is almost impossible these days.

Sadly, these advances in technology now mean that our children are not as effective communicators, and they need to learn new skills such as confidence and effective public speaking in order to perform well at job interviews and shine above the many other candidates.

ASSERTIVE OR BOSSY?

However, we don't want our children to fight their way to success but to shine their way. Some children from a young age are just natural born leaders. This can be seen as bossiness and can alienate our children from other children.

We need to explain to our children, in an age appropriate way, that other people's views and opinions are just as important as their own. And that everyone contributes something different and helpful overall.

At the same time, we still need to give our children those responsibilities that allow their light to shine and their leadership to flourish. They will need to be assertive in certain situations, but this is not a bad thing. If our children never asserted themselves, they would end up with what's left, or worse—nothing! Certainly not what they want or need.

It's not selfish to encourage our children to ask or go for what they want, as long as they are considerate toward others and are fair while allowing others to also do the same. And it's necessary they learn to speak up when they have to, or someone else will assert themselves and decide for our children what's best for them.

Some children are more introverted than others but that doesn't mean they can't assert themselves. It's not necessary to be loud and extrovert to get our point across, in fact, the quiet, calm approach is far more effective. It just takes confidence and knowing what we want or would like to achieve.

Regardless, in life there are always going to be leaders and followers, and when it comes to our own children, we can let them lead or be led, the choice is ours.

ENTHUSIASTIC OR HYPERACTIVE?

Children naturally have inexhaustible, high levels of energy.

This can be tiring for us parents, but it's just as draining for our children to be around us when we are tired.

Most of us either feel envious or admire other adults who seem to have boundless energy. We love to be around people who have an excited zest for life.

Yet parents and teachers alike sometimes feel the need to 'quash' that and calm children down (as we've learnt from my Son's red card incident over tambourine time).

Unbelievably, it's this kind of over enthusiasm, that makes children appear to be 'naughty', when actually, they are just excited or letting off steam and pent up energy.

Although, this energised state is normal, not abnormal.

Maybe it's time to observe our children who are full of life and let their energy rub off on us as we remember how we are meant and used to be, instead of trying to quash it.

HUMOUROUS OR CLASS CLOWN?

Another sought after quality in adults is a good sense of humour. GSOH is the one thing that all people look for in a partner and is ranked higher than attractiveness when looking for a mate.

This makes a sense of humour a very desirable quality to have. That is, unless you are a child with a good sense of humour that grownups just don't get!

Children who make a laugh and a joke out of things can be misunderstood. They are often seen as disruptive to teachers in school. Especially if they are clowning around amusing the other children when the teacher is trying to teach a class.

However, it's this same sense of humour that will help our children to be liked throughout their life and make friends and lift every body's spirits up in times of need.

Of course, our children's humour will probably be different from our own and may even sometimes seem a bit rude.

That's because that's what children find funny.

When they are entertaining their friends, we can either choose to overlook their innocent poo, bum, farting jokes, and rhymes about private bits (which they all enjoy at some stage because to them they're hilarious) or we can join in with the laughter.

Either way, it's best to let them laugh and be funny because humour is a desirable attribute. Children who can make other children laugh are popular, happier, and healthier.

Laughter is, after all, the best medicine!

OPINIONATED OR INTOLERANT?

Life can't always be full of laughs though, and throughout their lifetime, our children are certain to meet with conflict. Even if we never disagree with them or tell them off, someone else will.

I've encountered many very loving, well-meaning parents who never correct or reprimand their children. They just don't want to upset them in any way, but this ends up having the opposite effect in the long run. These children just aren't used to being challenged in any way, and they can't cope with it when it inevitably happens in real life. They may be intolerant of others as a result, believing no one should tell them anything, and believing they are always right, and when someone does challenge them or correct their behaviour, they take it as a personal attack and feel wronged in some way.

Some conflict can be useful, it teaches them that they can't always' be right or have their own way. It also encourages our children to stand up for what they believe in, teaching them how to form and express their opinions openly.

We don't want our children to become intolerant and small minded, but they still need to have their own opinions about life and feel free to express them with others.

Undoubtedly, others won't always share the same opinions. But If our children don't have the confidence to air their opinions, then they could repress who they really are. They may even feel that their thoughts and feelings are worthless to others. Resulting in a tendency to take on the views of others instead of their own. This can mean they back down and agree with anyone who expresses a difference of opinion to their own or compromise their own ideas.

This can lead to them becoming the 'Yes' men or women in society instead of becoming themselves.

It's healthy and normal for our children to encounter differences with others, they need to learn how to handle them. But if they are unable to tackle difficult issues or to challenge others, then they cannot learn how to resolve issues.

This way, they're unable to be true to themselves or anybody else for that matter, and will come to fear confrontation at all costs.

That's why it's vital our children are allowed to form and express their own personal opinions, regardless if we or others agree or disagree. And equally as important that we are not afraid to let them know it's just their opinion, not always a fact.

SELF-EXPRESSION

When we can recognise these often regarded 'negative traits' as our children's form of self-expression, then we no longer feel the need to try to change them or punish our children for them.

This makes life far easier for everyone concerned. It's not the easy option though. This approach is far harder for us parents to stick to than we might think.

Our children won't find it hard to be themselves and to express how they feel, but we will find it hard to manage that sometimes.

But our job as parents is not to manage our children but to love, teach, and accept them for who they really are, not who we or others want them to be.

The tactics that they employ are necessary to their development. If they don't let their feelings out any way that they can, then they can become depressed, frustrated, angry, or upset.

To help our children grow into adults who understand their own actions and the consequences they bring (even though they might not always be justified), we have to enable them to express themselves and help them learn how to deal and cope with their feelings.

When we can embrace their traits and understand the positive benefits they play in our children's overall personality and success in life, then we can help them to manage their own emotions safely, as well as other people's.

Expecting and accepting those traits and emotional states, along with some undesirable behaviour sometimes, can help us to positively and effectively manage their behaviour through love and learning.

CHAPTER 7:
THE ART OF POSITIVE, EFFECTIVE BEHAVIOUR COACHING

UNIQUE CHILDREN NOT BEHAVIOUR

WE HAVE SHOWN HOW unique our children are, but their behaviour, you may not be surprised to find, is not so unique. Parenting is the most important job in the world and the one thing that we don't want to get wrong. In fact, the implications of doing so are far reaching and can impact society.

That's why we desperately search for that quick fix solution to solve our children's behavioural issues. And why parenting books, classes, and TV programmes on managing children's unruly behaviour are so popular today.

We want answers.

We want solutions.

We want to find that one way to get it right.

Yet, parenting's something that we can only truly learn from experience, which includes trial and error.

There's no precise formula or rule book. Luckily, we make the rules.

Our children, despite their behaviour, are all unique.

And your child is no different to any other child on the planet.

Their fluctuating moods start from around twelve months of age. That's when they become emotionally labile and start developing their own sense of identity.

Their severe mood swings, toddler tantrums, and sulky teenage behaviours aren't anything new to the world of parenting. They are timeless problems that every parent faces.

Children have misbehaved this way for centuries. Even before they were freed from the 'Children should be seen and not heard' era.

Tempting as it may seem to go back to that time when children supposedly respected their elders, this would not be good for our children.

As a Mum, Childminder, and Therapist, I would be more concerned if a child never displayed any kind of unwanted behaviour. As this would likely be an unhealthy physical or psychological sign that something's wrong. Likely meaning the child was supressed and had given up trying to be who they really are.

Unwanted behaviour is not unnatural or uncommon, but our children are all different.

Each and every child we have is a genuine one off. No sibling could or should ever be the same, nor should our sisters, cousins or friend's children be either.

Accepting, allowing, and embracing our unique children with not so unique behaviour is how we begin to understand them. Once we can do this, then we can start to coach them as opposed to scold them.

COACHING

As already stated at the beginning of this book, rules are the key to managing unwanted behaviour, but they won't completely eliminate it.

The rules we make for our children provide instructions, but we have to teach them and coach them along the way. Discipline suggests we have to deal with and manage unwanted behaviour and then punish our children for it, but this 'Coaching' approach, is far more positive and effective long term. If we use any other methods, such as sending our children to the naughty step, then we need to ask ourselves, 'How effective will this method be when they are a teenager?'

Coaching is a longer-term method that's healthier than discipline because it's a more loving approach. It replaces punishment for training, teaching, and educating our children.

As we are aiming for happy, healthy, and successful children as opposed to perfect children, we are going to remain proactive in our approach and Coach them.

This means that we are going to pre-empt and prevent a lot of unwanted behaviour before it arises. Instead of punishing our children after the event when it's too late. We prepare them in advance by letting them know how we would like them to behave in certain situations. These lessons help them to understand what it is that we and others expect of them, which helps them to feel more confident, safer, and secure.

If you haven't read my other book *The Confident Parent's Guide to Raising a Happy, Healthy & Successful Child,* I recommend you do before you begin tackling unwanted behaviour. Having a routine in place will prevent a lot of undesirable behaviour and make rules easier to follow. Then we will be ready to go on to explore why our children misbehave and our options when confronted with their unwanted behaviour.

WHY DO OUR CHILDREN MISBEHAVE?

To help our children change their behaviour, we first have to understand why they are behaving the way they do. Like all good students, our children will make mistakes, and this usually results in misbehaviour or misunderstandings, either because they:

- Are angry that they can't get what they want or need.
- Are frustrated because they can't communicate what's wrong or what they want or need.
- Have misunderstood something or been misunderstood.

When they do misbehave, it's easy to see the behaviour as the main issue and to overlook the real reasons behind that behaviour that's causing them to misbehave.

There are normally many factors at play that contribute to our children's unwanted behaviour, such as:

- Lack of time with us.
- Sleep issues.

- Not getting enough exercise.
- Feeling unloved (of course they never are, but who knows what is going through their tiny minds)
- Not eating the right food at the right time.

Now, though, we will focus on miscommunication and how we can 'Coach' them rather than 'discipline' them.

MISCOMMUNICATION & MISUNDERSTANDINGS

Understanding that our children are not always being defiant, sometimes they're just misunderstood, enables us to want to help them rather than reprimand them.

We want to understand our children and we want them to feel understood. Otherwise, parenting can be challenging and childhood a scary, lonely, confusing time.

Misunderstanding in communication develops when our children don't know the rules of the game i.e. what is expected of them. As a proactive parent who (hopefully by now) provide routines for our children to follow, we are now prepared to address what our children want and need before they want and need it.

But this can pose a problem in itself.

When we try to pre-empt and prevent things occurring, sometimes, we can try too hard to analyse and find problems that may not exist.

The issue then is not always in our children misunderstanding what we want from them, but in us misunderstanding their age or stage of development. Which can be a challenge as these can be new to us and can change so often.

When faced with the unknown, it's inevitable that we will project our own thoughts and feelings onto our children. Unfortunately, these are often misinterpreted.

CRY BABY

Babies who cry offer a perfect example. They are not always crying because they are in pain, miserable, or to upset us. Although, this is an easy misunderstanding to make, particularly if we project what crying means to us onto our baby.

If we are concerned or confused about their crying, this can leave us wondering what is wrong with them and why do they cry so much?

Or what is wrong with us and what can we do to stop it?

These questions, along with the emotions attached to crying, can deter us from the real reason why our baby is crying.

We may fret and try to find out what is wrong with our baby, and when we cannot find the reason, we may wonder what is wrong with our parenting abilities and miss our baby's cues altogether.

Then, as our baby's communication is misunderstood by us, our baby cries more, and this becomes a perpetual cycle of miscommunication.

If our baby is constantly crying, it's safe to assume something is wrong. If they never stop, pain is the probable cause, and if you are ever concerned at all—seek medical attention straight away. Far better to get it wrong and be relieved it was only colic, than find out it's something more serious and you did not act on it. But generally, other than that, we need to understand that crying is just their form of communication.

They are communicating their needs to us by crying because they have no other way to let us know how they feel or what they want.

When we take the anxiety, frustration, and mystery out of crying, communicating with our baby becomes easier, and we are able to find the true cause of their crying.

Then they cry less, and we stress less. But until they learn to speak, crying is their only way to get our attention or to make themselves heard.

When it comes to behaviour, that's really all children are trying to do, get our ATTENTION and be HEARD. They just employ different tactics to do so.

They have to compete a lot for those two things. As parents, we are busy with caring for their everyday needs such as washing and ironing, cooking and cleaning. We may work too and also have money and relationship matters of our own, on top of that, we may have our own health issues to deal with.

Leaving our little ones to scream, shout, cry and possibly even hit out for our attention.

Even when we are spending time with our children, most of us aren't really listening. As a result, our children still don't feel heard. Misunderstandings can easily occur, that's why when it comes to communicating the rules, we have to make sure that they are clear enough for our children to understand and that they are set appropriately for their age. Expecting a baby not to cry or expecting them to share is not an age appropriate rule that they can understand. Distraction is a better method to coach babies and young children's behaviour.

PLAYING BY THE RULES

Making rules a fun game also helps, such as the 'Tidy up time game.' If we set a rule that our children must tidy up their toys when they've finished playing with them and we join in and compete with them to see who can put the most toys away the quickest, or if we have more than one child they can compete with one another, then children are more likely to accept and follow that rule.

And when we are in a situation that requires our children to be quiet, a game of 'who can stay silent the longest?' is always a really good challenge that children like to attempt. Believe me, children do actually love these games and actually ask to play them. We just have to be enthusiastic about them and make them fun.

Yesterday, I was doing a tea party for one of the children I mind, and one of the older children asked if they could play the 'see who could stay silent the longest game'. As it was a party, I had to say 'No' but I didn't argue over playing the tidying up game after the party!

In my setting, I'm lucky, as there's lots of children of different ages together. So, at the tea party, there were twelve children present, all wanting to stand out and gain positive attention. However, if you are a parent with only one or two children, some older children won't be fooled by games or distraction. These children are better suited to other methods.

MOTIVATIONAL METHODS

Being positive and supportive is the only way to help our children modify their behaviour. But no one method will ever work to manage our children's behaviour all of the time.

Each parent and child will behave and react differently from another. And each situation will be different too.

It's pointless then trying to learn the same strategy or set of rules and expecting the same set of outcomes for every child in every situation.

Common methods of managing or modifying behaviour such as stickers and charts work for some. Usually for those already conscientious children who are motivated by rewards. Other children on the other hand are motivated by not losing something that they already have, such as their favourite toy. And some, just can't be influenced by anything.

What works for one child, will not necessarily work for all. So, we have to think about what personally motivates our child before implementing anything. Always taking into consideration their age, stage of development, personality, likes, and dislikes.

DON'T STICK WITH IT OR GET STUCK!

One Mum I worked with used a sticker reward chart for all three of her children. Although, not one of them had ever been good enough to get sufficient stickers for a reward.

Despite this, she stuck with this method that didn't seem to be working for years. Even though the age range of her children varied from seventeen months to ten years of age. The youngest was too young to understand the system, the oldest too old to be motivated by a sticker, and the middle child, who probably would have been suited to that method the most, saw that the other two children took no notice of it and so followed suit.

As well as that, the goals that she had set for her children were not achievable for all of them. And, as none of them had ever received a reward, they could not see the point of it all. They were demotivated instead of motivated because she failed to notice that each of her children were different, not only in age, but in what motivated them.

THE SECRET TO MOTIVATION IS A MOTIVE

Given a good enough reason, our children will be motivated, especially to do those things that they like. Other times, they may need a little convincing and a reason why they should cooperate before they do it.

'That's why' won't motivate them. We need to be a little proactive in our approach. Maybe the incentive of pocket money if they tidy their bedroom will?

Knowing what motivates them and choosing our words wisely when asking them to do something, will make all of the difference to the outcome.

If, for instance we, want them to do their homework but they are absorbed in another activity, demanding they do it because we say so will not motivate them. Especially if they are enjoying what they are doing. But if we rephrase it by explaining that once their homework is done, they can then carry on doing what they enjoy uninterrupted, and maybe even stay up an extra ten minutes before bedtime, we might encourage them. Particularly if we point out how happy their teacher will be when they hand in their homework on time, spurring them on some more when they realise the benefits for them.

BLACKMAIL OR THE ART OF NEGOTIATION?

Older children tend to prefer the 'Play by My Rules and I will Play by Yours' art of negotiation. For example, if they want to go to the cinema Friday night with friends, then they must first do their homework.

Then if they want spending money to take, they must also tidy their room by Thursday.

One parent once said to me that they didn't like the idea of blackmailing their children, but I don't see it that way.

When I work every day, I would rather look at it as exchanging my services to earn a reward that benefits both parties. Instead of seeing it as I'm being blackmailed.

Children need motivation to do those things in life they don't want to do. This is what prepares them for life in the adult world. Negotiation is a currency that older children will understand and will keep them motivated to follow the rules.

After all, what we are asking them to do, i.e. their homework, in exchange for going to the cinema with friends are both of benefit to them, not us. Whether we agree with it or not, we need to get good at it, and get some practice in now.

Our children will spend their teenage years negotiating with us all the time, and we have to show them that it works both ways. Negotiating is a fine art. And our skills of negotiation will need honing over time just as positive, effective behaviour coaching is an art that needs honing too.

WHY IS POSITIVE, EFFECTIVE, BEHAVIOUR, COACHING AN ART?

Our children are not always intentionally trying to misbehave. They only do so as a natural part of growing up. They are experimenting and developing their own points of view and ideas while discovering who they are and what they want or do not want.

The problem with this is they are always changing and developing. We not only have to keep up, but we have to find new ways of dealing with their new phases and behaviours.

The trick to mastering The Art of Positive, Effective, Behaviour, Coaching is to understand this and:

- Firstly, expect conflict regardless of what we do. If we expect it, we can prepare for it. This way, our proactive approach to handling our children's behaviour will be more effective.
- Secondly, no matter what our approach to dealing with our children's behaviour may be, we have to realise that by making our children feel bad, we will never be able to make them act good.
- And thirdly, understand that it is an art because it's not something that we can instantly learn from a book or a friend. It's a skill that we learn, develop, and hone over time.

If we started doing something new, such as learning how to play a musical instrument, after only a couple of years we would not expect ourselves to be as good as Mozart. Naturally talented or otherwise, we all learn and improve over time in any endeavour, and parenting is no exception.

We mustn't beat ourselves up for not knowing how to manage unwanted behaviour or for not having all the answers. Until we find what works for us and our children, all we can do is keep calm, confident, and carry on.

In the meantime, our rules and routines that we want our children to follow will support us along the way. First, though, we need to know how to positively communicate them so our children will want to willingly follow them.

STAY POSITIVE

The only way we are going to be effective and positive in coaching our children's behaviour is by remaining positive ourselves.

In the assumed words of Gandhi: 'Be the positive change that you want to see'

Any rules we set should be positively stated because our children are unable to process negative commands positively.

If we say to them 'Don't think of your Bed Time Bear.' Every time they will think of their Bed Time Bear. This is because they have to think about the thing that they are not supposed to think about first in order to process our request in their mind. Instead of telling them what we don't want them to do, we need to give them instructions on what we do want them to do or how we want them to behave.

'Be good like you normally are' is far better than saying to them 'Don't be naughty like you normally are.'

Presupposing using 'normally are' sets out our expectations of them. To positively affect our children's behaviour, we want them to concentrate on what we want by using positive words and phrases.

Words are really powerful. Every time we tell them 'You are always naughty,' we reinforce that behaviour.

'You always play nicely with others' or 'You are kind' are therefore better suggestions to give.

Children are very susceptible to suggestions; we are literally hypnotizing them with our words.

That's why we need to word what we say in a constructive, positive way before we speak. As the saying goes, 'If you don't have anything nice to say, then don't say anything at all'.

We are more accustomed to telling our children what we don't want, so changing how we speak may be difficult to begin with.

If it is, we can be sure that's a good sign that we are making progress as we begin to notice those negative words more and more.

Whereas before, we may not have even noticed that we were speaking negatively to our children.

This new awareness prompts us to change how we phrase things from negative to positive. Then, over time, using positive language will become automatic as it becomes positive Auto Pilot Parenting. Then we won't need to think about what we are saying or how we speak to our children so much.

This awareness can also help us appreciate how hard it must have been in the past for our children to change their negative behaviour when the instructions they had received from us were negative.

EXAMPLES OF NEGATIVE TO POSITIVE

Here are a few negative to positive examples to try.

Instead of saying:

- 'Don't spill your drink.' Try, 'Keep your drink in the cup.' The first instruction 'Don't spill your drink' is registering in our children's minds as they are concentrating on their cup as 'Spill drink', but the latter request 'Keep your drink in the cup' keeps their focus on the drink staying in the cup.
- 'Don't run around.' Try, 'Let's sit here for a moment, it won't be long before it's our turn.'
- 'There's nothing to be afraid of.' Try, 'What would your favourite Superhero do now to help them sleep?'
- 'Don't pee on the floor.' Try 'Keep your wee, wee in the toilet, there's a good boy/girl.'
- 'Don't eat your food in the living room.' Say, 'Let's eat the food at the dining room table like we are supposed to.'
- 'No hitting.' Try, 'We don't hurt one another, it's nice to be kind, isn't it?'

We are suggesting what it is they should do, and offering them questions that bring them to positive answers. When we explain how we expect them to behave in plain language that they can understand, they are more likely to want to behave well and try to please us.

No child ever really wants to misbehave and be told off, it's not a nice feeling.

There will always be occasions when our children will misbehave and when it may be necessary for us to tell them off. This is because it's not natural for them to follow what we want and conform.

If we demand they stop crying, running around or shouting, their natural instinct is to cry, run, or shout. These commands to stop are unnatural to children, and their emotions can be uncontrollable.

We can try to teach them self-control, but we need to take into account that it's not a natural or easy thing for them to do. Children do what is natural to them at the time.

If they are upset, regardless if we feel the reason is justified or not, they will struggle to hold their tears and tantrums back. Their brain is not developed enough to do so. Exercising self-control is again another art that they too will need to hone over time as they grow up. We just have to be positive, patient, and understanding with them until then.

TERRIFYING TODDLERS AND OTHER CHILDISH BEHAVIOUR

Very young children, such as those 'Terrifying Toddlers', can't control themselves. Can't be controlled by others. And can't always understand rules and routines to begin with.

We have to be patient and persist with our rules and routines until they learn them.

Until then, as parents, we have to stop trying to stop or control their tantrums.

As long as they are not harming anyone, including themselves, we can feel free to just leave them to it while they tantrum it out of their system.

We should never avoid people, places, or situations through fear of the dreaded tantrum.

If we do, this means that our children's behaviour is controlling us.

We have to show them that we are not going to be controlled. If we are worried that they may misbehave or embarrass us, then we will never be able to coach them in public positively or effectively. Fear and embarrassment are the main culprits for many parents losing control and shouting, smacking, or nagging relentlessly.

We are not perfect parents (no one is) but as Powerful, Proactive, and Present Parents, we can allow our children the freedom to tantrum.

If we remain calm and unphased, they will soon learn that there's no point in carrying on anymore and will act appropriately.

We just need to watch their nonverbal and verbal cues to warn us when a tantrum is about to erupt. Often, the best thing to do is offer a gentle distraction while we try to figure out what is behind that particular episode and how best to communicate with them.

If distraction fails, then we can simply do nothing except acknowledge to them we are aware that they are upset. While letting them know that we cannot help them while they are having a tantrum. Reassuring them that this frightening reaction they're experiencing will soon end and we will be there to talk to them and try to help them when they have finished.

Then we can either watch unphased, or if it is safe to do so, we can walk away and wait from a distance and let them tantrum it out alone until they come to us for a cuddle afterward.

Our children fight for our attention any way that they can. If the negative approach doesn't seem to be working, they'll soon come to us for some love.

When they realise they are not getting the attention that they desire, they will soon become bored and stop of their own accord. We shouldn't take it personally though or hold a grudge against them. It's a childish way of venting their frustration, but it's the only way that they know how to.

Misbehaviour and tantrums are just signs that can help us to find the source of the problem. If we can treat them as clues as to how our children are feeling, and find out why they feel this way, this can better help us to help them.

These outbursts can be very valuable in understanding and connecting with our children. As long as we can be proactive and take them in this way instead of trying to stop them or ignoring them.

HUG IT OUT INSTEAD OF TIME OUT!

As proactive parents, we try to prevent situations escalating. Emotions can seem to come from nowhere, but they really don't. They gradually build up, so noticing the warning signs and helping our children deal with how they are thinking or feeling, before they lose control, is vital. Naughty steps and time out are auto pilot parenting solutions to unwanted behaviour that solve nothing. We are, in essence, reacting after the event, when it's too late. Our involvement as proactive parents is to pre-empt and prevent always. Using time out, naughty steps, and chairs is a lot easier than pre-empting and managing unwanted behaviour because this all takes time, patience, and unconditional love. To love our children when they are trying to hurt us, others, or themselves is not easy.

When we find it difficult loving our children unconditionally, it's because we have changed, not them though. They haven't suddenly become unlovable because they've done something we dislike. We've become conditional in the way that we show them our love and affection. To love unconditionally, we need to act lovingly, despite the absence of good behaviour.

Unconditional love never tries to score points, intimidate, blackmail, scold, hold onto resentment, grudges, or induce guilt in any way. We have a duty to correct our children if they genuinely upset us, and under no circumstances should we ever give in to their challenging behaviour or tantrums to get their own way. We must stay strong, committed, and calm. This is best done by explaining how we feel, in a loving manner, from a place of teaching, and nurturing our children, not punishing them.

Time out and naughty steps are not effective in coaching or teaching our children. Yes, they remove our children from a situation, yes, they segregate them from those they love, yes, they can humiliate, yes, they can produce feelings of guilt and worthlessness and make their anger or fear worse. It's no secret that they can be very successful in making our children feel bad, but as we know, we can never make our children behave good by making them feel bad.

Our job is to help our children build self-esteem, to feel they are good and worthy so they form a positive self-image of themselves, but if they are sent away alone, this only serves to reinforce their unworthiness and unlovability, and that image soon takes a negative shape in their mind.

We think that by removing our children, we prevent ourselves auto pilot parenting and being driven by our own emotions, but just because we have breathing space, we can't assume our children will go away and cool down too. We may imagine they will ponder the error of their ways, think about what they've done, and come back when we say, feeling remorseful and sorry and apologise, and all will be well again. But the reality is, when we leave them alone with their thoughts and emotions, they become even more upset, afraid, isolated, and angry.

We can't help our children when they are wrapped up in rage. Hurricane Tommy, or whatever your little one is called, will be on self-destruct, and whatever or whoever is in their way will get swept up in their emotions too. Chatting at this point in time is futile—they can't hear what we are saying and quite frankly they won't care—the talking and teaching must come before the storm. All we can do is be there to help them manage themselves and be a beacon of light in a dark place for them to turn to in the midst of their turmoil.

When they hit out in anger or meltdown in a pool of tears, we know they need us most. We can't abandon them when they need comfort, reassurance, and answers. Yes, they want to know and understand why they feel the way they do.

They are seeking answers always and need explanations as to how their behaviour has impacted those around them and what they can do in the future to prevent feeling and acting this way, because children are frightened by their uncontrollable emotions. The naughty step, seat, or time out is not a magical solution that transforms our children from little devils to angelic angels. Only we as parents have that kind of power and influence over our children. Everything over time loses its sparkle, and the naughty step is no exception, what may have seemed like a powerful solution in the beginning, soon turns into the norm. Children can become resigned to it, and I've known of children who sit themselves on the naughty step without being asked when they know they've done something wrong. It's a bit like being absolved of the crime or guilt by means of confession. And I've lost count of all the children and times that 'sorry' has been said as if it's a magic word that puts all wrongdoing right. Saying sorry helps, but it's just a word that gets conveniently used as a get out of jail card, eventually lacking in any meaning. Instead of preventing repeated unwanted behaviour, it ironically ends up reinforcing it because children think as long as they get punished and say sorry that it's okay to behave inappropriately.

Also, if a child is used to a certain naughty spot that they get sent to, in time, that spot is where they will just go to escape situations, a hiding place that has no meaning. We all have an inbuilt survival mode known as the fight or flight response, it's where adrenalin pumps through us in times of perceived danger and we either prepare our body for a fight, freeze still, or we run away. The naughty step encourages this running away from problems and challenges. If the anxiety or fear is strong, the reaction is, 'Let's get out of here'. But the problem with this is we can't run from ourselves and our emotions forever and we don't want to teach our children too either. Far better to face our fears, and that way, they dissolve naturally and appropriately and there's less chance of them repeatedly rearing their ugly head again. (We will cover this in depth later on in 'Get your own emotions in check!')

When they are in their hiding spot, we may get exasperated even further if we see our children messing about and acting as though they don't care about what they've done or how they've behaved.

But this is often their way of distracting themselves from their emotions and coping with their unwanted behaviour, they don't know any other way until we show them. That's why communication is so important. Talking and listening is what will make situations better, not ignoring emotions or having time alone to think. What do you think our children are actually thinking about when they are in time out?

Probably how much they hate us for getting angry at them and how awful we are or how unfair their life is, or, if they are really smart, reasoning with themselves that what they did was justified at the time.

We have to find ways to proactively involve our children in the process of managing their emotions. By making our children part of the solution today, we equip them to understand and manage themselves in the future. This potentially removes unwanted behaviour in the future. Remember, our children can be part of the problem or solution. We are not going to eradicate tantrums and unwanted behaviour, but how we approach it and involve our children in resolving it, is what makes all the difference.

TOMMY VS JOHNNY

Let's say toddler Tommy has hit baby Johnny on purpose because baby Johnny was holding Tommy's favourite Teddy and wouldn't let it go. Auto pilot Mummy may smack or shout at Tommy and say 'You're the big Brother, you should know better.' But obviously, Tommy didn't!

Now, Auto pilot Mummy has reinforced hitting or shouting to resolve conflict.

But Tommy still hasn't been taught how to share. That was the lesson there that auto pilot Mummy completely missed. She could've taught and coached Tommy by explaining that Johnny was a baby, who, like Tommy, doesn't understand the concept of sharing and that certain toys belong to certain people.

All Tommy knew and was interested in was it was his favourite Teddy not his little brothers, and he wanted it back!

Johnny didn't want to give it back though, so Tommy would do anything in his power to reclaim his beloved possession. And he did, he hit out. Proactive Mummy would have first made a fuss of baby Johnny who was hurt, not a fuss of toddler Tommy.

If at this point Tommy was sent to the naughty step as punishment, he wouldn't have been able to see the repercussions of his actions, i.e. baby Johnny crying, hurt, and upset and Mummy showering him with love and affection. Unless Tommy is a psychopath (we'll assume he isn't, as all young children are simply just selfish, and he's too young to get saddled with a damaging label!), then seeing his brother hurt as a result of his actions would be upsetting for Tommy. If he was stood observing the aftermath, he would probably feel upset he had hurt his brother but would also wonder why is Baby Johnny being lavished with love when he was the one who started all this by pinching my teddy!

Cue proactive Mummy's chance to explain and teach Tommy, once baby Johnny had calmed down and was okay.

It's frightening for a toddler to see how he can actually hurt someone he really loves, and at first glance, to auto pilot Mummy, Tommy's reaction looks deliberate, as if he wanted to hurt his baby brother. But despite what morally he thought was right, it was his teddy after all, it wasn't intentional, he hasn't developed morals, this is something he'll learn from his parents and being in these uncomfortable situations. The truth of the matter is, he simply couldn't control his emotions.

Instead of ostracizing Tommy and sending him to the naughty step or giving him a label such as naughty or bad boy, proactive Mummy needs to involve him and show him that she loves him, but his behaviour was not appropriate. It's proactive Mummy's moral duty to make it clear that Tommy must never put his hands on anyone and to empathize that she understands he was hurt that Johnny had his favourite teddy, and she knows why he reacted the way he did, but hurting someone else because he feels hurt doesn't resolve things, it makes it worse. Giving him examples helps him to make connections with how his actions make others feel, for example, explaining to Tommy that what he had done was not acceptable and that baby Johnny now feels hurt like that time when_____, then filling in a blank with a time when Tommy was hurt and upset. This invokes empathy. He may cry as he realises what he has done was wrong. He's learnt a powerful emotional lesson here. This is proactive Mummy's cue to offer a little reassurance, such as a kiss or a hug.

This way, she demonstrates that it's okay to get angry and have these emotions, they are not bad, they are trying to teach us something, and that she accepts that he was angry and that happens sometimes, but there are other ways to release that anger. So next time he feels that way, he can come and talk about his feelings. This helps open up a channel of future communication.

On the other hand, he may still not see that what he has done was wrong, so, as proactive parents, we have to be on the lookout for any repeat behaviour again so we can reinforce that lesson until he gets it.

We also need to encourage him to make it up with his baby brother, maybe kiss baby Johnny better to show his affection and forgiveness, which is important. Having a family group hug makes Tommy feel forgiven and included again and Johnny feel better too, and as a parent, peace and love feels restored. Next time, try hugging your child a couple of minutes longer than usual and feel the love transmitted back and forth. That's our bonds strengthening and reconnecting us to one another. When we have strong bonds, coaching becomes easy, our children want to listen and learn from us, they trust us.

Coaching behaviour shows unconditional love, a naughty step shows our love comes with conditions.

I know I've said all this in my previous book as love is the major part of my U URSELF Routine, but it's fitting to repeat my point again here. Anything other than unconditional love will feel like hard work because it usually relies on our children meeting our expectations, which is always going to be difficult.

Unconditional love means that no matter what our children do or don't do, say or don't say, it doesn't affect the love that we feel for them. Even when we feel as though they've let us down, those are the best moments to practice unconditional love, and there will be many of them. When our children need discipline, this may seem the hardest time to give them our love, but it's the time they need it most.

If they say, 'I hate you,' we can counteract it with 'I love you.'

If they do something wrong, we can give them a cuddle instead of telling them off while we explain right from wrong lovingly.

It's not about overlooking what they do wrong, letting them have their own way, or giving in to them. It's about freeing ourselves to love unconditionally so that everyone feels good. You'll know the difference between naturally occurring, unconditional love, and trying to force love.

Anything other than the former will be a constant, tiring, struggle, making us feel, guilty, anxious, drained, angry, frustrated or unhappy.

Love is all that ever matters in our relationship with our children. Nothing else is as important as unconditional love, ever. If it feels like hard work, then it's not unconditional love. If we are trying to restrict, control, or have a hold on or over our children, it's conditional love. It feels like we are enduring our parenting role. We need not endure unconditional love but enjoy it. It's a freedom. It's an allowing. It's a letting go.

When we are unconditionally loving parents, then we will have equally loving children. Being loving satisfies a basic need within all of us.

Once we realise that our children are neither good nor bad, they are just being themselves in each and every moment, and we can stop judging them, we can then truly love them unconditionally. From this unconditional loving position, we no longer need to excuse our children's behaviour or feel embarrassed by it.

It's only a form of self-expression at that moment, and it's okay.

We want them to love themselves, but if they feel bad or naughty all the time, they'll find it hard to do this, wondering what's wrong with them.

But there's absolutely nothing wrong with them, how could there be?

At birth, they were a blank slate, free from everything; they were born perfect in every way.

When we accept and approve of them, they will accept and approve of themselves. Making them more inclined to respect others and less inclined to hurt, humiliate, or compete with others or turn to any outside influences.

When we are ill, our body cries out in pain to let us know that something is wrong and needs our attention. It's the same for our children's tantrums, they are our children's way of trying to tell us they need help with something that they can't cope with alone. When they turn to others instead of us to help them, that's when we have real problems.

CHAPTER 8
OUTSIDE INFLUENCES

I T'S TIME TO UNCOVER in this chapter the 'outside influences' in our children's lives that can sometimes seem out of our control.

As our children become older, it's more important than ever not to take our eyes off the ball (or off our children so to speak).

As they age, we need more than ever before to proactively keep up with them and stay in the loop. Spending much of their time away from us once they start school and make friends, it's easy to lose touch of what and who is influencing them.

As soon as friends become a big influence in their lives, we start to notice our children changing quite dramatically.

THAT'S WHAT FRIENDS ARE FOR

While young, we still have a certain degree of control over who and what our children are exposed to. Unfortunately, as they grow up, our involvement and influence slowly decrease. There's not a lot we can do to prevent this other than locking them away in their bedroom for the rest of their lives without any contact with the outside world.

As this would cause more harm than good, it's best to become more proactive and involved in those things we still do have influence over in their lives.

It's understandable that as parents, we want to shield our children from outside negative influences. The problem though with trying to control all negative outside influences is that:

A. It's impossible to do; and
B. We end up controlling our children and parenting on Auto Pilot mode as a result.

Influences can include other people such as extended family, friend's, romantic relations, teachers, nannies, childminders, celebrities etc...

All of these will have a profound effect on our children's personality. That's why it's important we are aware of what or who they are being influenced by.

The more we can positively influence our children while they are young, the more likely our children will be to regulate their own influences from the outside world when they are older.

We can monitor those 'other people' in our children's life who could potentially be role models such as grandparents, aunts, uncles, cousins, and friends. Ensuring our children spend their time around those who serve as positive role models and less time around those who could serve as undesirable ones.

But what we can't really do is choose our children's friends or family.

When they are young, we can have influence over their playmates as we organise and arrange our little one's activities and outings and tend to socialise with our own friends and their children—ones we get to pick.

But once they start childcare or school, it's by chance who they get on with and why.

This shouldn't matter too much as children are innocent when young with the main aim of just having fun!

This friendly influence can sometimes change when our children start primary school. This is when friends become even more important to our children's wellbeing and emotional and mental state. As they move through the infants, they generally gravitate toward a group or a friend who likes to play the same games as them or who shares similar interests as they do. Then when they reach Junior School, they start to form real friendships.

However, these usually change again once they reach high school and meet new people, or when friendship becomes more discerning and taken more seriously.

Although we can do a lot for our children, we cannot be their best friends, no matter how hard we try.

Our sense of humour will be on a completely different wavelength to theirs. And we can't help but to see life from a grownup perspective. While our children without experience can't possibly view life from our point of view.

As adults, we have the added advantage of having gone through what they are going through. Yet we learn so much from our experience and forget so much that usually, we can't relate to how our children are thinking or feeling.

Along with our different ideas, goals, and motives, all of this means that it's hard to ever understand each other fully, let alone share the same points of view.

Whether our children think we are wrong or we wonder if we are right, no matter how much we love and respect them or doubt ourselves, we are their leader always.

Despite other outside influences, we need to stay confident and calm at all times and enforce rules and boundaries for them to follow.

All of this is hard to do on an equal footing as a best mate. Because parental love can sometimes mean tough love such as making them go to bed on time or even depriving them of a mobile phone!

FRENEMIES

Friends, on the other hand, play such an important role in teaching our children the lessons that we can't.

Parents don't want to be the ones who have to show their children all those negative emotions such as jealousy or anger. That's not the role of a loving parent. But friendships involve handling those uncomfortable emotions.

Although these may not seem like positive experiences at the time, especially when they cause our children to fall out with their friends, they are all vital in helping our children to learn and grow.

Even when their friendships evoke anger, jealousy, rejection, betrayal, aggression, fear, and sadness. They are all important emotions for children to encounter in order for them to learn how to deal with them, in both themselves and in others.

Children can't learn how to cope with these types of emotions by explanations alone. They have to experience them first-hand and understand how these emotions make them and other people feel. That's why enemies can become our children's best friends or frenemies.

But more than that, friends can help our children to become the people who they truly want to be. Not who we as parents wish they would be.

Although we only ever have our children's best interests at heart, more often than not, these interests are biased and are based on what we want for our children.

We may want them to study hard at school in order to pursue a professional career, but our children may have other dreams for their future such as backpacking around a third world country, helping others out as a volunteer.

Although we would be justified in pointing out the dangers of such a pursuit, we would be biasedly influencing them. Where friends, on the other hand, may encourage them to follow their dreams.

This is another reason why we cannot be our children's best friend. Our roles as parent and offspring can make it difficult to be truthful at all times with one another. Our motives maybe different, and our children may not always be comfortable confiding in us.

This could be for many reasons, such as they may:

- Worry that we have enough worries of our own without them adding to them.
- Feel embarrassed to discuss with us feelings they may have for another person.
- Fear of our disapproval about something or someone.
- Have an issue relating to us that they feel we won't be able to see or understand from their point of view.

None of this should disappoint or worry us though because that's what friends are for, providing an unbiased, listening ear with empathy, not sympathy.

A friend needs to be someone who can understand what our children are going through. As parents, it's great if we can try and understand what our children are going through. But knowing what's cool and what's not and sharing experiences that are current to them is something only a friend who is of a similar age or in the same situation can do. These are roles that we can't always fulfil.

What we can do is be the best parent that we can be and let our children find their own best friends who they can turn to for advice and support.

We can always offer our children our counsel and guidance, but as they age, we can expect them to be too embarrassed to be seen out in public with us oldies, let alone confide in us or ask us for our advice on boys, girl's, careers, or fashion.

Rest assured, though, this phase doesn't last. As they mature and leave their teens, they will soon return to us for assistance once again. When they discover that:

- They didn't really know it all after all!
- We were not always wrong!
- Not all of their friends were always giving them the right advice!
- We were not outdated in our ways and beliefs, just experienced in the way of the world!
- What they thought was fashionable, we were wearing twenty years before them and it's not us who were old fashioned after all!
- The pop music they now listen to is a rehash from our era and was probably taken from a classical piece of music before our time too!
- We only ever had their best interests at heart!
- We love and care for them, more than anyone else in the world.

Until then, all we can do is accept the inevitable, growing up, rebellious process. While we wait and prepare to pick up the pieces and make it all better when they do come back to us.

MAKING FRIENDS WITH THEIR FRIENDS

In spite of this, as Proactive Parents, we still need to make sure that we take an active interest in outside influences. Especially their friends. This is what makes us Powerful Parents.

It's important to build good relationships with our children's friends because these friends can work for or against us.

Even if we don't particularly like them (in fact, *especially* if we don't like them), it's a good idea to invite them over often and make them feel welcome in our homes.

The saying 'keep your friends close and your enemies even closer' applies here when it comes to the interest of our children.

Paying particular interest in sudden changes in friendships and new best friends. Particularly in: How? Where? When? And why they met them?

It's just as important we try to find out what has happened to their old friendships and why too?

These answers will enlighten us on the direction our children are taking.

If our children make and keep friends easily and they already have good friends that stand by them, then they won't feel the need to fit in or to be influenced by others. This may well prevent them from getting in with the wrong crowd. But, if they feel left out, lonely, or they don't get on at school, then they are open to falling into bad company.

This is when there is a potential risk of them joining gangs to fit in or form friendships or relationships that place too much peer pressure on them.

We can't really change our children's friends and choose new ones that we approve of but we can monitor those they do have along with other outside influences.

We may not understand, accept, or like our children's choice of friends. But we can try to be thankful anyway that they have friends who they like and who they can get on with.

Friends play such a valuable role in our children's life. That's why it's important that we can help our children make and keep friends while also keeping an eye on the ones we don't want them to keep too.

It can be difficult for us to accept other outside influences, as in preschool, our children are influenced by ourselves or other family members. Giving us as parents the exclusive power to censor what they are exposed to and pick up to a certain extent.

This disappears once they start school though, when the majority of their time is spent away from us. This is when we start to feel our own sense of influence and power slipping and when their individuality takes form and their ideas and outlooks on life change, often conflicting with our own. But this is not always due to friends.

THE OTHER INFLUENCES

Unfortunately, the influences that will have the greatest impact these days are likely to be the digital type.

The media, including social media, is one of the biggest outside influences we should start paying attention to.

The remote gaming community, the party chatrooms, social media, TV, magazines, newspapers, films, computer games, music, books, or vloggers, bloggers, and YouTube sensations on the internet are not as easy to monitor and keep track of.

MEDIA – PG – PARENTAL GUIDANCE!

Films and games are very influential, so it's a good idea to pay attention to what our children are watching or playing. To help us in deciding what is suitable for our children, films and games, by law, have legal age ratings.

This is to ensure a minor cannot buy inappropriate material. But it's our responsibility as parents to ensure they do not watch inappropriate material.

PG means just that, parental guidance. It means we need to watch the content beforehand or alongside our children and decide if it is going to be suitable and age appropriate for them. PG doesn't mean it's a kid's film.

Children mimic the actions and behaviours they see. And any violent material, children tend to copy. This has sadly been proven all too often when children have committed serious crimes by copying what they have watched in a particular film that they should not have been watching.

We must teach our children while they are young to know that these age restrictions are there for a good reason. That way, when we are not around to sensor what they watch, they can decide for themselves what's appropriate and will know what they are not allowed to watch.

We can be Proactive Parents by not buying or allowing our children to read, play with, watch, or listen to anything that is unsuitable for their age. We can also set up child pins on our satellite TV's and child restriction software on our computers that prevent them from accessing whatever they want.

It's an unsettling fact that children are now accessing explicit material on the internet freely. Now, I'm sure teenage boys were looking for the magazines on the top shelf when I was at school way back when. But the age and nature of what children are exposed to today is far younger, more graphic, and real, so we have to ensure we use filters to block this explicit content and set controls and privacy.

Many parents and children just don't realise that YouTube has an age limit of thirteen. Yet toddlers watching cartoons on there have become common everyday occurrences. Lots of parents I have spoken to hadn't even set their preferences to safe mode as they didn't realise there was the option to do this. For more information on this you can read the NSPCC's guide on Help Keep Children Safe Online and Share Aware.

We have to have rules around what apps or sites our children are allowed to access and when?

We also need to be aware of what our children are being exposed to at their friend's houses too. Essentially, making our views on age restrictions clear beforehand when we know our children are going to spend time at friends or extended families' houses.

Innocent Cartoon Characters

Many popular super-hero films and computer games have quite high age restrictions that many of us parents may be unaware of. Just because our children wear the pyjamas, watch the cartoons, or play with the action figures does not mean aggressive games or films with violent or sexual scenes are suitable.

Check out the age ratings on some of your children's computer games, phone apps, or films, and you may be surprised to find how high they actually are.

Our children's friend's parents may not mind their children watching or playing them, but we shouldn't take that as an indication that the content is suitable for our children.

We must always take into consideration the maturity and understanding of our own child, regardless of other people's views or opinions.

Even when, maturity wise, we consider our children to be advanced beyond their years, we still should adhere to the age guidelines.

We are protecting our children. We're not being overprotective by not allowing them to watch, listen, or play, anything over their age rating.

We are being responsible, proactive parents, preventing problems for our children, both now and in the future.

SOCIAL MEDIA

Even if we make a conscious effort to sensor what our children watch, read, or listen to, there are so many other ways the media can creep into their lives. And with social media growing ever popular, our children are being exposed to unsuitable material at even younger ages than ever before.

As parents, we feel under immense pressure from our children to set up social media accounts or download apps. Yet again, many of us are unaware of the age that children are allowed to join social media, such as Facebook—which, incidentally, is thirteen.

And we seldom check an apps age rating or creator.

Those terms and conditions and fine print are skipped, skimmed, or unread as we are being nagged and reminded of all their friends or younger children they know of who already have them.

Social media may seem like a harmless, fun way to communicate, but again, there's a reason for the age ratings. Children are too naive to understand the world of unknown people hiding behind social media masks.

And they are certainly not mature enough to deal with the graphic content it typically contains. Not all of which is true, but to a young impressionable person who believes everything they see, hear, or read, it can be scary stuff.

Social media forces our children to grow up before their time and to be exposed to content above and beyond their age that they simply are not ready for.

There is no rush for our children to hurry up and grow up, but only we can encourage them to savour their childhood.

As parents, we are the only ones who can help to keep our own children as young, innocent, and carefree as possible for as long as possible while we still have the power to do so.

EMMA GRANT

THE CHANGING STATES OF PLAY

Childhood is short, and playtime now is shorter than ever.

Although keen to grow up and become independent, children are just growing up too quick for their age.

These days, children are encouraged to grow up and stop playing with toys. Having access to their own computers, phones, and satellite TV, it's now the norm to follow pop music, vloggers, celebs, and the current fashion trends more than it is to waste time playing childish games.

Although play has changed a lot over the last twenty years, we should still be encouraging our children to play creatively and to role play with dolls and action men, not iPhone's or iPad's.

Children shun action figures in favour of virtual war on a computer console that are more vivid and real, and nothing is left to the imagination. And sadly, children are no longer roleplaying with dolls, now they are actually dressing up and potty-training real babies before they've matured enough.

I know this sounds far-fetched, even frightening, but it's true, and, sadly, it's accepted as normal.

Over the last sixteen years as a Childminder, I've witnessed many different states of play. Still, even I'm dumfounded by the switch from imaginative play to digital play. My children and those I cared for at the beginning of my career loved using recycled household rubbish such as cereal boxes and toilet roll tubes to make things and messy play was a thrill such as papier mâché and making homemade playdough. I myself as a child spent many hours making mud pies in the garden, but now, children as young as three are carrying handheld computers and phones around with them and are now disgusted by sticky playdough or paint, asking to wash their hands or have a wet wipe before we've even begun!

Children just don't know how to play creatively anymore.

It's time to let our children be children once again. Allowing them the privilege to play and have a carefree childhood, fuelled by their own imagination, not hypnotised by computers like robots.

Only we can encourage our children to play and to enjoy the present age and stage they are at. We need to convince them that there's no rush to grow up. After all, it's us parents who decide how fast they grow up. Yes, all their friends may have a mobile phone, but who gave them one in the first place?

If we could all as parents, stand united and enforce age restrictions at home onto social media, mobile devices, games, and films, then peer pressure from friends to play or have the latest phones or computers would not exist.

Realistically, though, that is never going to happen now. Once they pass seven years of age, friends are such powerful influences in our children's lives.

And, hands down, what their friends do and have is always going to be cool. And what we do and say becomes less cool as our children age. Cool... Is that still even a word? My teens would argue not, it's just not cool to say cool anymore.

All we can really do is try to proactively put our children off the latest advances in technology as long as we can.

STORIES & RHYMES OF SCARIER TIMES

I'm not saying in 'the good old days' way back when, life was perfect. Far from it. Different times pose different problems.

We had our fair share of doom and gloom. Especially if we consider some of the traditional bedtime fairy tales we were told as children that portrayed the world as a frightening and dangerous place.

It's a miracle we ever slept at night listening to *Hansel and Gretel* and *Little Red Riding Hood* to name just two horror stories. These Wicked Witches and Wolves who eat frail old Grannies is enough to give any one nightmares.

They definitely gave children the message that it's a big, bad, scary, world out there, occupied by villains and nasty people. And let's not forget those innocent, sweet, nursery rhymes that have been passed on to little ones for generations. Do you remember the words to Three Blind Mice?

Is it any wonder then that many of us grew up accepting bad news as normal when it was fed to us as babies?

If these stories and rhymes were before your time, then lucky you! But you may want to research them on the internet anyway to see what I mean. There's nothing wrong with nursery rhymes per se, many of us grew up listening and learning from them. I still find many of them useful tools in my childminding practice. Luckily, these days, stories and rhymes tend to be less harsh and more politically correct. But even this has been taken to the opposite extreme.

In their time, these rhymes were teaching children history, and although the messages today are somewhat outdated, children still enjoy dancing to nursery rhymes such as 'Ring A Ring o' Rosie', oblivious to its history or metaphorical value.

As of the time of writing this, I'm forty-two year's young. In my relatively short time on earth, I've seen the world dramatically change, certainly since I started writing this book ten years ago.

And now, there are many good children's books out there, written by positive, motivational authors such as the late Louise Hay's, *The Adventures of Lulu* or inspiring books by Dr Wayne Dyer such as *Incredible Me* or *No More Excuses*. All of these portray positive, life affirming messages. They also help our children to deal positively with the real problems in life too.

NO NEWS IS GOOD NEWS!

No news is good news, as they say.

We may be led to believe that it's educational and informative for our children to follow the news because it allows them to know what the world is really like, but how often do you see or hear good news?

Does that mean that in reality there is no good news?

And no good people or experiences in the world, only bad?

Does the daily news really offer our children a balanced, realistic view of the world?

Or does it just highlight all the doom and gloom to sensationally sell more newspapers and boost ratings?

Unfortunately, bad news sells!

It's what the majority of people like to hear about. It's debatable whether the Pollyanna Gazette would be as popular?

Fortunately, life is not all doom and gloom, but if our children are being exposed to bad news every day, then they may start to believe it is.

In fact, they will likely become accustomed to it and expect bad news, associating more with it than any good news they may hear.

We should take care to protect our young, innocent children's impressionable minds. Regular exposure to such negativity could cause nightmares, and some sensitive children could become fearful, sad, or depressed.

We do not, however, need to hide the truth from our children or try to protect them from hearing about anything unpleasant. Quite the opposite, it's actually beneficial that they are aware of both the good and the bad news.

Yes, bad things happen in the world but so do good things too. We just need to give our children a more balanced outlook and show them what's good about life more often than highlighting the bad news.

There are people experiencing poverty and tragedy in the world, even today, but our children do not need to feel sad, fearful, or guilty because of that. It's not their fault. Our children have a right to be happy, regardless of what's going on in the world. Undoubtably, they will have a hard time being happy and carefree if they are aware of all that's going on, which is out of their control.

If they want to make a contribution to society and a positive difference in the world, our children will have to learn how to free and empower themselves.

Something they can only do if they feel good. It's hard to be an up lifter when you're feeling down or fearful. This is where we can positively help to direct their attention on good causes.

Some people may think that you can't shelter your children from the real world, scary stuff happens every day and it's happening more and more. Not reading about it or watching it on TV won't make it go away. I totally agree, but watching and reading about it won't change anything either.

Just as exposing our children to scary stories can cause anxiety and fear, it's pointless to highlight it unless we are willing to address the problem. Children do worry, they magnify things, and they don't understand life as we do. When they hear there's a murderer on the loose, even if that murder is in a different part of the country or even the other side of the world, they will have nightmares of the murderer coming to their house to get their family. They just won't understand the back story. Maybe the murderer killed someone he knew on accident and has no intention of hurting anyone? But that won't matter to a young child.

As a childminder, I've had to reassure and calm many a child down over something in the news that was bothering them. One child was petrified of a tsunami washing their home and family away and desperately didn't want to go to school in case it happened.

As a therapist, one of the first things I advise my adult clients with anxiety to do is stop listening to the news. It's amazing how that one simple thing makes them feel better in such a short space of time.

Taking a proactive approach and preventing our children getting caught up in bad news and taking action to personally change the world positively when we can will yield the most beneficial results.

Spreading love, joy, and happiness instead of doom and impending disaster as each individual person, one by one, we can impact those around us. Starting with ourselves by being a good role model to our children, then coaching our children's behaviour positively, is what will make a difference to society as a whole.

We can't change other people, but we can and do affect them negatively or positively.

As an influential role model, you decide.

It's a sad fact that we have become numb to horrific news. In America, children and gun crime is considered an increasing occurrence, and in the UK, we face a children's knife crime epidemic, and somehow, now it's become normal—like old news. Something needs to be done fast to help our children, as well as other children, realise there is another way to behave, and that love is their right.

We can't solve hate with hate, we solve it with love, understanding, empathy and support.

At home, we have the opportunity to talk to our children and to teach them right from wrong and the value of every individual person's life on the planet. If our children are fortunate, we teach them not to condemn or judge but to reach out to those less so. Often, being a friend who listens is enough, that's what children want most—to be listened to and understood and to have friends and family that care about them. Unfortunately, a lot of children don't have those fundamental, basic needs met on a daily basis. The frustrations arise when no one is listening and a child feels abandoned or misunderstood.

How we parent does make a difference to the future news, as well as who our children admire and look up to in the media.

CELEBRITY INFLUENCE

Again, it doesn't mean we can choose who our children look up to or like. We probably won't agree with their choice of pop icon or the type of music they listen to, but neither did our parents with us, or our parents', parents with them. It's inevitable that our children will find iconic celebrities to look up to or aspire to be like. Especially with such an influx of TV reality shows where anyone can now attain celebrity status simply for being outlandish. Unfortunately, for our easily led children, like some friends they may encounter, not all of these celebrities will model desirable behaviour.

SOAP & POP!

An overlooked source of influence is of course these reality shows, soap operas, and pop music videos. They may not be extremely violent and the swear words may be bleeped out, but the content is sometimes inappropriate for children and often of a sexual nature.

Next time your child is watching a soap opera or music channel, think about the seemingly innocent messages these images are conveying to them. And anyone who's watched these reality shows would know—there's little left to the imagination.

If we can turn these negative influences into positive ones by helping our children to learn from other people's mistakes, then this could prevent them making the same mistakes themselves. With my own teenage daughter, I explained if you do watch these popular shows, observe how going out on the lash and sleeping with random strangers transpires in the show. There's always tears, heartbreak, regret, and fighting! And usually alcohol fuels recklessness and poor judgement.

By showing our children these celebrities making mistakes that ruin their careers or personal lives, we help them to understand the negative consequences of such irresponsible actions. It's not that we want to judge or discredit anyone, but demonstrate that for every action there is a consequence.

This lesson can easily be forgotten, no matter how many times we explain it to our children. It's one of the first lessons and certainly most important lessons, to coaching our children's behaviour. Therefore, any opportunity we have to highlight it is a plus for us. There's always a moment between making a decision and acting on it where our children can consider the consequences of their actions if they act on them. By instilling this in them from a young age and reinforcing it throughout their childhood and teens, they will automatically form the habit of thinking first. This lesson requires constant repetition on our part, so we have to be like a stuck record, as the old saying goes, until their brains develop enough to do this for themselves. This will serve them well in their adult lives. However, it won't prevent them ever making mistakes, having poor judgement, or being led by strong emotions or hormones. But when we can highlight the fact that not everyone does the right thing or acts the right way, no matter who they are or what they have, we help our children understand that not all celebrities are positive influences or people to be admired, despite millions of social media followers or dollars in the bank.

They are just normal people. This insight may discourage our children from copying negative role models and encourage them to take from each person the positive characteristic's that they admire the most and be themselves. Learning to be themselves and love and accept themselves is important, as parents we can only go so far in helping our children, they play the most important part themselves. That's why allowing them the chance to grow and become the person they want to be by loosening the reins and stepping back and giving them the freedom to be themselves is crucial. As we've explored in how to make the perfect child, being themselves should come naturally, yet with so much influence and input from others, over time, they may find being themselves is not so good. Especially if they've heard negative suggestions from others, in particular—authority figures, such as teachers and parents or influential peers. Then they try to change themselves to fit in or to become accepted by others. This can be damaging to their self-esteem and can affect their self-confidence in all areas of their lives, sometimes creating unhealthy habits.

CHAPTER 9:
POWERFUL PARENTS

THE MOST PROACTIVE THING we can do to influence our children is to be a positive role model ourselves for them to follow.

As we've discovered, we're in the perfect and very powerful position to teach our children whatever we wish them to learn. Even though we may not have all the answers and be perfect parents, we can still be positive, influential role models for our children to follow.

Undoubtedly, they will copy others and have many other role models besides us throughout their lifetime. From cartoon characters to celebrities, school teachers to friends, but we are their first and most influential role model of all.

FOLLOW THE LEADER

Like it or not, whether we help or hinder our children along the way, positively or negatively, we are powerful leaders in their lives.

We can and do, to a certain extent, determine the direction that they go in. Therefore, it's best to make that direction as positive as possible if we want our children to be happy, healthy, and successful.

If we believe that there is a right way for our children to behave, then we have to bring them up and show them the right way according to our beliefs.

WHO INFLUENCED YOU?

Talking to our children about our own experiences and how others have influenced us in our lives can be very illuminating for our children. Having an insight into who we are and why we are the way we are helps them to better understand us. And both people in any relationship being understood is key to happy, loving relationships built on trust and honesty.

But who influenced you to become the person and parent that you are today?

Somebody did.

Every person that you have come into contact with up until now has influenced you in some way. And each were important in making you the person and the parent you are today.

Before we can positively influence our children, it's a good idea to identify who or what has influenced us in our own lives and understand how that has affected us today in our parenting roles.

You can probably easily recall the famous people such as athletes, writers, actors, or pop idols that influenced you growing up.

But how about the people who personally made an impact on you and your life such as parents, grandparents, aunties, uncles, cousins, siblings, or friends?

Consider for a moment the following questions:

- Think back to some of the important people in your life, and try to identify how they influenced you.
- Did they help or hinder you emotionally, financially, educationally, socially, physically, environmentally, motivationally, or spiritually?
- What attributes or qualities did you admire most about those people who influenced you the most?
- What traits or bad habits did you dislike most about them?
- As a child, did you aspire to be anyone else other than yourself? If so, who and why?

You may find it difficult to pinpoint just one person, or easy to identify one strong, influential person in your life.

No matter how big or small an impression, all that matters is that you can see how others have influenced you in the past in becoming the person and parent that you are today.

If like most, you will have encountered a variety of people, all with different influences in your life. And you can encompass and use all of that to draw on in your parenting role today.

However, in order to help you become a positive influence in your child's life today, the experiences or people themselves in your past don't have to have been all positive.

In fact, you will have probably learnt the best lessons from the negative ones.

Even if our own parents were not particularly good role models to be around or if in our past, we have not been the people we wished we were. Here and now, our children present us with the perfect opportunity to change all that.

No matter how negatively we have been influenced in the past, we can act differently toward our own children today than how we were treated. Any negative parenting endured as a child gives us perfect examples of how not to parent our own children. It's actually the best motivation we can have to be a better, more positive, influential role model to our own children.

SO, HOW ARE YOU INFLUENCING YOUR CHILD?

So, how are we influencing our children?

If you want to discover how you are influencing your child, their behaviour may not be a good enough indicator. You could, of course, ask them for their opinion if they are old enough. Brace yourself though, children can be brutally honest if asked for their opinions, but if we want them to be honest and open, we have to allow them to be.

Or you could just try the following exercise, which is more enlightening and fun.

BEING YOUR CHILD EXERCISE

- Close your eyes now and imagine what it is like to be your child.
- Visualise Stepping into their shoes or crawling in their nappies for a day and notice what it feels, sounds, or looks like to be them.
- How do you think they feel being your child?
- What do you understand about yourself, as a parent, from their perspective?
- How do you see yourself influencing them emotionally, educationally, socially, financially, physically, motivationally, or spiritually? Are you a good role model to them in all these areas?
- If your child's old enough to understand the question 'How do they think you are as a role model?' would you ask them?
- If not, why not? What are you afraid they may or may not say?

A REWARDING RESPONSIBILITY

As such influential role models to our children, it may feel daunting sometimes, carrying all of that responsibility for someone else on our shoulders.

Equally, it's also very exciting and rewarding to be able to mould another person into a happy, healthy, and successful individual.

Literally, in our hands we have the opportunity, potentially, to raise loving individuals who become valuable assets to society.

I'll say this again, this privilege is not something we want other people to take credit or responsibility for, and certainly not worth risking to chance.

Being honest about the things or people who negatively influenced us could encourage our children to avoid the pitfalls of worshiping the wrong type of person or engaging in risky activity. By sharing our experiences and views, instead of telling them what they should or shouldn't do, discrediting or dismissing their idols, we are offering them constructive guidance. Not judgemental criticism.

This way, they are more likely to accept or listen to our advice, rather than us telling them who they should or should not like or listen to.

CHOOSING POSITIVE ROLE MODELS EXERCISE

Discussing our own role models and why we admire them and how they inspire us today can be a great source of inspiration for our children to find their own positive role models too.

We can help them with this, but we have to make sure that we find people who interest and inspire our children, not ourselves. Then invest in books they have written, magazine articles about them, or if we are able to, buy our children tickets to their shows or events.

There are plenty of good, positive role models in the world that we can encourage our children to aspire to, from Olympic athletes to noble prize-winning scientists. A fun way to do this is to encourage our children to create a scrap book about their favourites. Including inspiring and motivational pictures and interesting information printed out from the internet or cut out from newspapers, magazine interviews, and articles on their chosen person.

We could turn this into some fun Us Time together and extend this activity by doing the following exercise:

- Get some newspapers and magazines and cut out pictures of celebrities, politicians, and athletes etc. then, with your child, each make a pile of people that you like, respect, and admire and another pile of those people you do not like, respect, or admire.

- Then take it in turns to choose a picture and discuss with each other what you either dislike or like about the person. Notice how your views and opinions, likes and dislikes differ from one another. But do not judge or criticize your child's views or opinions and make sure they don't do the same to you. The exercise is to point out what you like or dislike in others, not in each other. It's about discussion, not debates or arguments. Remember, you need to respect your child's point of view as important, and vice versa if you are to positively be of any influence to them.

It's useful to know what attributes our children find admirable in others, as this can give us an idea of what they are aiming to be like themselves.

It's also useful in helping us to model those desirable aspects in ourselves too. If our children find aspects in us that they admire and respect, again, we will have a better chance of positively influencing them. This will be an invaluable asset when trying to manage their behaviour and gain their respect.

Our children learn how to behave and respond to others and situations from observing and mimicking us. That's why this book has spent so much time looking at our own behaviour before trying to modify our children's.

The realisation by the end of this book, hopefully, will be that by changing ourselves and becoming the parent we want to be, we will see the child that we want to see.

MIRROR IMAGE?

When we look in the mirror, who do we see?

Our children are a reflection of that image, so it's pretty important we get to know and like ourselves more.

All of our personal morals, opinions, and beliefs are passed onto our children and become their own. Just as many of our own have been passed onto us from others, such as our parents.

We can get a good indication of what type of example we are setting by the values, integrity, and beliefs our children hold and the behaviours they express.

If we find that we do not like the way our children are thinking or behaving, or we believe they're lacking important principles, then we need to check if we are modelling those principles and behaviours clearly enough in ourselves?

It's a bit like looking in the mirror when we are overweight, we may try to convince ourselves and others into believing that we do all the right things, Such as eating healthily and exercising, but if the reflection looking back at us in the mirror and the rest of the world tells a different story, we have to ask ourselves why.

When we look at our children, it's just like looking at our own reflection in the mirror. How we view ourselves has a huge impact on how our children view themselves.

If we look in the mirror for our imperfections and insult ourselves, then, eventually, our children will do the same to themselves. Likewise, if we find positive things to say about ourselves and appreciate our good features, they will recognise their own too.

Children learn from copying us. Mirroring, as it is termed, scientists have proven, comes instinctually with children and parents. It's also a skill which comes naturally when in rapport with another person.

This is not a conscious effort. Our children naturally observe and record everything that they learn from us to ensure their learning and survival. Going back to the brain wave states we discussed earlier in thinking more childlike, children absorb everything in their theta state under six years, it's learning that takes place directly in the subconscious, and the subconscious is really what runs our lives. It creates our habits and how we respond to circumstances. Therefore, if we overreact to something such as a bee buzzing past us and jump around screeching and shouting, waving our arms in a panic, our children, in their heightened, frightened state of alertness, will record the incident as dangerous and develop a fear of bees and will react similarly to us every time a bee comes near them. But if we stay calm and still and say, 'how beautiful, a busy bee,' there's less chance of that bee retaliating and stinging anyone and less chance of our children overreacting in the future to bees.

We can be sure that either way, until they reach their teens, whether they copy us consciously or subconsciously, it is our influence that they are mimicking.

That's why it's vital that first we must be the person we want our children to become ourselves before we try to change their behaviour in any way. And this is not always easy, as this requires walking our talk.

WALK YOUR TALK

You could say as parents, it's our job to set a good example for our children to copy. They trust us and believe in what we do and say. That's why we need to make sure that we are trustworthy and someone who's worth believing in.

Our actions and opinions have a huge impact, not only on the way that our children think and behave now, but how they will in the future.

That means the repercussions of how we think and behave, positively or negatively, can affect generations to come!

Which is why being present in the moment as parents, and reflecting on ourselves, is vital when it comes to our actions, words, thoughts, and feelings. Although they copy our physical actions, words, and mannerisms, children also learn a lot from our non-verbal body language, including our general unspoken thoughts and feelings on life.

It's a good idea to make our daily mantra, 'Practice what you preach and live what you teach!'

I know this is not always easy, but the more conscious as parents we become, the easier it will get!

As our children are constantly listening and watching us, we need to model the behaviours we desire in our children in ourselves all of the time. Being a positive, influential role model is not something that can be done only when convenient then neglected at other times.

Our children learn everything from us. That's why to be of any real positive influence we have to live the life that we want our children to live as well.

If we want them to be healthy, then we have to practise healthy habits ourselves. Such as eating healthily and taking regular exercise. We also need to demonstrate how we want our children to act. This means that if we want them to be kind and loving to others, we too should do the same.

This way, they learn from us appropriately how to:

- Get along with and cooperate and communicate with others.
- Respond and deal with conflict.
- Manage disappointments.
- Apologize.
- Be loving, patient, and considerate.

Whatever we expect of our children, we must be willing to walk our own talk and do so our self. In theory, this may seem like a no brainer to many of us, yet in practice, it may be very difficult to do at times.

Our children don't only learn from what we say, but also from what we do, or as the case may be, what we don't do.

Therefore, it's not 'Do as I say' that will influence our children but 'Do as I do'

If we want to be proactive in our approach to parenting and be a positive influence in our children's lives, then by our own example, we need to show them the benefits of a good routine and a healthy lifestyle.

This way, they are more inclined to want to willingly copy us. This may mean changing some old habits and practising new, more positive, life enhancing ones instead. Such as replacing fast food for fruit and vegetables, alcohol for water or smoking for exercise.

Whatever changes we need to make, we have to make sure our children see us being happy, healthy, and successful before we can expect it of them.

Our own health, happiness, and success teaches our children how to be healthy, happy, and successful. A teacher can already do what they ask of their student, a preacher usually can't!

TEACHER NOT PREACHER

This is the difference between a teacher and a preacher.

We all want the best for our children, yet we contradict what we teach them by how we act.

This can lead to us preaching to them the opposite to how we actually live our own lives.

To find out if you are preaching or teaching, ask yourself the following questions:

Do you:

- Have a career you love or a job that you hate?
- Have good friends who you trust and enjoy spending time with, or two-faced, gossiping acquaintances who you moan and complain about?
- Act responsibly, such as saving your money for the things you want, or do you spend money you don't have on things that you don't need?
- Do you choose to practice healthy habits or indulge in addictive behaviour?
- Act self-confidently and display high levels of self-esteem or shy away, feeling victimised by other people or life?
- Act lovingly to your partner and family, or do you argue and criticize them all the time?
- Worry and get down and anxious, or do you relish each day as an opportunity to have the best day ever?
- Get envious or jealous of others, or do you positively encourage and support others and celebrate in their successes?
- Feel tired all the time, or do you bounce out of bed and throughout the day with a spring in your step?

Asking ourselves these types of questions is not always pleasant, yet beneficial when it comes to evaluating what kind of role model we are really being to our children.

If some of your answers did not make you feel like you were being a positive role model, then don't worry. None of us will tick all of the right boxes all of the time, simply because we are all human. But now that you have noticed the areas that need attention in your own life, you can do something positive to change them.

It's when we don't notice, or we deny them or blame other people that we encounter problems. This leads to the difficult task of convincing our children to do as we say, not as we do.

We should always encourage positive attributes like honesty and forgiveness in our children, but if we don't show we also possess them, they won't want to either.

We can't pretend for long, our overall attitude to people and to life is transparent in all that we do. When we try, we only end up confusing our children with our conflicting words and actions. These mixed messages contradict what we say with what we actually do. For example, it's pointless telling our children off for hitting another child if we smack our children when we feel they are being naughty. They are only copying the behaviour that we are modelling.

As parents, we have a duty to act appropriately. If we enjoy getting drunk and dancing on the table, then that's fine for a Saturday night out with friends. But at a children's party, it's not an appropriate example to set. From a health and safety perspective alone, it's inappropriate, but from a powerful parent's position, when it comes to telling our children off for standing on the furniture in the future, we won't have a leg or table to stand on!

The thought of our children imitating our behaviour or turning out like us when they are older can be a scary prospect for some.

It can also be the wakeup call we need to change the way we are influencing our children and the prompt to take action in becoming a role model that we are happy for our children to follow.

It's not about being perfect and never making any mistakes, it's openly acknowledging them when we do.

It's becoming more present by stopping to think about what we're about to do or say before we act or speak. So that whenever we are about to do or say something that we wouldn't want our children to do or say, we stop ourselves.

This gives us the time to question our reasons why we wouldn't want our children to copy us.

And to ask why we are choosing to behave this way ourselves.

Such as, why wouldn't we want our children to get ridiculously drunk and smoke thirty cigarettes for fun?

If our answers suggest it's because we don't want our children to end up hurting themselves or others, then, surely, we should want the same for ourselves too.

We condone certain behaviours by our own actions. If we smoke, for instance, our children just won't understand or even believe the concept that smoking can kill them.

Instead they will naturally assume that if we do something, then it is safe for them to do it too.

After all, why would we do anything that wasn't good for us? they'd think.

It can be difficult to stop ourselves doing things that we know are bad for us sometimes. Especially if it involves addictions, but it all comes down to practising integrity in the moment and having a big enough why or why not to motivate us.

PRACTISING INTEGRITY IN THE MOMENT OF CHOICE

Integrity in the moment of choice means that if our goal is to be a positive influential role model to our children, and we feel the need to do something we wouldn't want our children to copy, then we choose to make the decision not to do it.

If we refrain from doing something that we wouldn't want our children to do, then we pass on to them a valuable lesson. That is, we walk our own talk at all times and have integrity.

That builds trust on both sides.

And if our children can trust us, chances are, we will be able to trust them too, and we won't have to worry about them sneaking off to do things behind our back either.

Exercising integrity in the moment is not just about those things we don't want our children to copy though. It's also about doing what we say we will do and maintaining our children's trust by keeping promises.

If we promise to take our child to the park but unexpectedly our friend pops in for coffee, this means we keep our promise to our child and still take them to the park. Even if it means we go slightly later than planned after our friend leaves or even asking our friend to come with us or to call back another time.

And if we make a promise to someone else that doesn't directly involve or affect our children, we should still demonstrate our integrity. The decisions we make or promises we keep to others show's our children that we are a person of our word, and they will come to respect that.

It's good to have a degree of flexibility in life but not at the cost of letting our children down or damaging our own integrity in the process.

By always being true to our word with our children, we help them to build trust and faith in us.

This way, we can feel confident that we are doing the right thing, at the right time, for the right people, for the right reasons.

It's not about compromising, pleasing others, or giving in to our children's demands.

It's about responsibly sticking to our integrity in the moment of choice and doing what we said we would.

HONESTY IS THE BEST POLICY

However, no matter how much integrity we have, it's inevitable there will be times when we will, for whatever reason, break a promise we make or end up letting our children down in some way.

In those instances, honesty is always the best policy.

We can help teach our children a valuable lesson if we don't cover things up or lie about them.

When we are truthful with our children and explain our reasons why we had to break our promise, they learn to understand that things don't always go to plan, and that's life!

But we can also prevent a lot of heartache and issues to begin with if we only make promises based on what we know we can honestly fulfil.

We must never be tempted to make empty promises that we have no way or intention of keeping. We have seen previously in this book what can happen when we go back on our empty threat and allow our children to go to a party that we said they wouldn't go to because of their behaviour. Being honest with what we can physically do for our children is the same.

If we promise our child that we will get their bike fixed by tea time but don't know how we are going to fix it or have other commitments, such as work all day, this would be an impossible promise to keep.

We are, in essence, setting ourselves up to fail and creating tears and tantrums later on.

If we cannot or do not want to do something, it is far better to let our children down immediately rather than later on.

'We'll see' or 'maybe' are popular parental phrases that our children take for granted as a 'Yes' we will do something or let them have something.

We need to be very careful with these loose teasers, they can sometimes backfire on us.

A 'No' now saves tears and tantrums later on when we eventually get around to telling them the truth.

It's far better to endeavour to keep promises and be open and honest to begin with. Then we can proactively deal with the issues today, instead of the problems tomorrow.

Although we will always encounter problems, and instinctively we will want to protect our children from the truth sometimes. But keeping things from our children to protect them can also backfire on us. The truth usually comes out in the end, one way or another, to cause havoc.

However difficult to do, it's healthier to be open and honest with our children and to talk about our feelings. While also responding empathetically, when our children open up to us too. We may feel they don't need to know all the details of a troubling situation, but often, the truth is far better than their imagination. So, if we don't fill in their blanks or talk to them openly and honestly, then they will fill them in for themselves. This way, they may end up blaming themselves for things that have nothing to do with them.

When it comes to parenting, honesty really is the best policy, even if it doesn't always make us look or feel so good at the time. Our children learn more from our honesty than they do from our lies.

We can't deny how we are feeling all the time—our emotions have a way of showing others how we are feeling inside.

And it's unrealistic to pretend that we don't make mistakes. They are part of learning and growing, so we don't need to feel embarrassed, ashamed, or afraid to admit when we are wrong or have made a mistake.

It's good for our children to know that we all experience strong emotions at times and that it's not only themselves who make mistakes—as adults, we do too, and that's okay. You probably know by now that a positive role model is someone who can:

- Identify their emotions.
- Admit their mistakes.
- Learn from them.
- Change them into positives.
- Help others to do the same.

GET YOUR OWN EMOTIONS IN ORDER FIRST

Wouldn't it be insightful if we were able to identify, understand, and express our own emotions before helping our children deal with theirs?

This means managing our own feelings and behaviour appropriately first before expecting our children to be able to manage theirs. Instead of hiding or fighting our emotions, we use them as a resource to help guide us and understand ourselves. We have to be free to express them instead of fearfully hiding them, while at the same time, having the awareness that how we express them impacts our children. Remember that they acquire their responses from observing us. How we deal with challenges, sadness, fear, anger, or change will be reflected in our children's behaviour and how they learn to deal with those things.

A lot of mental health issues are due to not being able to face our emotions, or by us supressing them either consciously or subconsciously or distracting ourselves with other things. They never go away though. Being present in the here and now is difficult for most of us because when we are still and quiet, we can hear and feel those thoughts and feelings buried within us. Being busy keeps us safe from the truth of how we really feel.

Children's therapy is one of the most googled things on the internet, and it's ever present that our young are experiencing more and more anxiety and mental health issues at an earlier age than ever before. And I know from my experience as a therapist that most of the issue's adults come to see me with stem from childhood. This is why we need to address or prevent issues proactively while our children are young so they don't end up being the adult clients on the couch later on. These problems seem to repeat and accumulate over time until they come to a head, or the person can no longer take the stress that's built up. The message is this, catch those emotions and let them lead to the source of the problem so we can resolve it before it grows and manifests into a monster. Modern life is getting increasingly complex, boundaries in all areas are getting more and more blurred every day, this is a problem that without early intervention is just going to snowball.

Being proactive in our approach to parenting will prevent a lot of unnecessary issues occurring for our children, but equally, we need to address ourselves to be effective.

It's a team effort, but when you can acknowledge and accept your feelings, you can focus on the present moment and see the situation, whatever that may be, for what it is. If you and your child are both in an emotionally charged state, the best course of action is to change the environment.

This doesn't mean running out of the supermarket, dragging your kicking and screaming child behind you in a fight or flight response to anxiety and going home to escape. It means taking your child gently by the hand and suggesting that you both go for a walk around the carpark for some fresh air.

Maybe also suggesting a game of counting all the green coloured cars as we walk and see if we can find at least ten?

This way, we're teaching our children not only counting and colours, but more importantly, we are diffusing a situation by teaching our children to stay present on what's around them in their environment and not allowing them to get lost in their emotions or own mind. Then, once everyone's mind is a little clearer, we can return to doing the shopping in a more relaxed state. We are, in effect, teaching our children an alternative way of resolving conflict. We are demonstrating a healthier approach to dealing and managing emotions, it's definitely a more loving way when we coach not reproach our children. We hate seeing them upset and angry, and they too feel the same about us. But we have to remember they only behave the way that they do because they know no other way to respond unless we show them. This does take time, patience, persistence, practice, positivity, and the ability to stay present. Once we master these five little P's in a pod we can really help our children. But we must coach them continually to condition them in the appropriate ways.

When we can listen to our emotions and keep them in check, we grow and learn. We call this emotional intelligence, it's what puts us in touch with how we are feeling, and it provides valuable teaching opportunities for our children.

E.g. Lily, do you know why Mummy is so angry?'

'No?'

'Because you broke the rules or moved the boundaries of what we agreed, I said that you do not go outside the garden gate, and you agreed. But you went outside anyway where there is a very busy road full of fast-moving traffic where you could have gotten hurt.'

Of course, we don't want to tell our children off for 'what ifs' that haven't actually happened, but going against the agreed rules is why we are explaining. If, at this point, we lose control of our emotions through fear, anger, or frustration and smack them, they get physically hurt not by the car on the road but by us! The only lesson they've learnt here is fear. By explaining that we love them and were only upset because we were worried for their safety because of the potential dangers is how our children learn. Now Lily is learning why she has made her mother angry, instead of her just getting upset at her mum's anger toward her, she's questioning in the present moment how her past actions have caused this situation, making Lily more self-aware, giving her time to make connections in her head, relating past, present, and future information. This way, the next time Lily goes to do the thing that has made her mother angry in the past, she will be able to retrieve this memory, and if her mum has explained appropriately to her in the past, she'll understand why her mum will be angry with her again for repeating the unwanted behaviour in the future.

If, however, Lily is always used to receiving a smack every time she does something that her mother disapproves of, she just learns that smacking is the answer to every problem, and later on in life, this will become her modus operandi, i.e. her habitual approach, meaning, her m.o. becomes physical violence. Every reaction we have toward our children's behaviour becomes etched in their memory bank. The more intense the emotions at the time, such as the angrier we are and the more upset our children become, the more significant this event will seem on reflection.

My Dad is still haunted by his father smashing his wireless radio on the fire grate when he was younger. It didn't physically scar him, but sixty odd years later or so, it's still an emotionally charged memory for him today. He felt repressed and afraid, and this impacted his life later on in many ways.

But we must understand that many childhood memories and their associated feeling, such as fear or anxiety, is based on the perspective of a child, i.e. if they are three years old when a traumatic event occurred, then even at ninety-three, they may still recall that scenario with the same intense feelings as they did as a three-year-old. That's why some grown men are petrified of spiders. Shouting at your child for something that may seem trivial at the time, may not feel significant for you, but it's how your child interprets the situation and from their young person's mind how they perceive things that will determine its significance in their lives later on.

Maybe you and your partner are arguing over something trivial such as whose turn is it to take the rubbish out or wash the dishes, things may get heated if one of you is frustrated that the other one isn't pulling their weight around the house. It's not anything serious enough to warrant divorce proceedings, and you and your partner both know that. But enough of these minor disputes can cause your child fear and anxiety. Being mindful of how our children interpret reality differently from us is key. It's what helps us to manage our emotions and reactions effectively.

Although, keeping your emotions in check does not mean ignoring them or supressing them or distracting yourself with work, household chores, or comforting addictive habits such as smoking or overeating. It's allowing them to surface and looking at them as an observer, from that vantage point you can ask:

'What is this emotion trying to tell me?' Or, 'What's the underlying message that I am avoiding?'

E.g., you are angry at your child, you can't ignore that anger, but you can notice it and acknowledge that because **you** are feeling this way does not make you a bad parent just because you get angry at your child. You are normal, but keeping that emotion in check means you don't react inappropriately toward your child, such as shouting or hitting them out of anger. Maybe you haven't noticed yet, but If you do act in anger, you end up with more unwanted emotions such as guilt and sadness afterward which serve to add to the initial problem. Remember, you are not an angry person because sometimes you feel angry, just because we are angry at our children for something they have done, doesn't make us unloving parents either. An hour later, we may be praising them and showering them with love.

Our behaviours and emotions change from moment to moment. They are in the moment strong feelings, but like every other moment, they too pass, then the anger dissolves.

As long as we are aware of them, we can be the loving parents that deep down we all are through our conscious moment to moment choices.

But we can't decide to be a loving parent one day and that's it, we can never get angry or upset ever again.

That would be acting something that we are not, and suppressing or denying our true feelings is pointless as emotions always manifest in one way or another eventually.

It's best to allow ourselves to be and feel as we choose, but not to think that is who we are or that we can't change.

Moment by moment, we can all change and be the loving parent we choose to be, regardless of our past actions or behaviour.

The way we act is transparent to children, they may not always question us on a conscious level, but deep down, they know and understand our true feelings.

We can't act one way and say something else or say something and act differently. Our actions need to correspond with our words.

It's the same with being a loving parent, it's not something that we have to learn or change about ourselves.

It's not something we do or do not have; it's who we are, or who we are not.

We don't do something in particular to suddenly become a loving parent; we just are loving at that moment or not. We have the choice when we become Present Parents.

As we are so transparent to our children who pick up not only on how they see us behaving but also on how they feel our emotions (yes, our energy radiates outward and our children pick up both our good and bad vibes), then what we don't want to do is transfer our emotions, fears, and anxieties onto our children. If we suffer the slightest anxiety or doubt, it will be reflected in our body language, tone of voice, and the words that we use, causing our children to feel anxious and doubtful also.

Yes, we are allowed to be upset when it's appropriate, such as when we have lost a loved one, that's a natural expression, but being angry and upset over a spilt drink is another matter. Keep them in check!

Likewise, we may have anxiety about going to the dentist, but being anxious because our children are going to the dentist is a different story. They look to us to lead, protect, and reassure them. We need to be careful not to overreact or transfer how we are feeling onto our children.

As a first aider, we are taught to prevent unnecessary fear, shock, or trauma, and that we must stay calm and positive with a casualty, even if we can clearly see they are in a bad way, we can't convey that to them, or we could affect how they recover.

Note how a child who falls over and scuffs their knee will either bounce back up and carry on or burst into hysterics crying, depending on how the parent reacts. If a parent rushes over anxiously and looks horrified at the slightest sight of blood, that fear will scare the child into thinking a little graze means something terrible and serious. They need to feel reassured that everything's okay and feel secure that we are taking them into situations that are in their best interest, not scary places that could harm them in some way. The dentist is, after all, there to help keep them healthy, not to hurt them.

We need to convey to them how we want them to feel. If we want them to calm down, we need to remain calm. If we want them to have self-control, we need to show them how to do it by controlling ourselves.

When we learn to take responsibility for our own feelings, our children can learn that emotional literacy from us.

Our emotions are helping us to learn and grow, they provide us with feedback, they are like red flags in the fast-flowing sea of life, change course, swim to the shore, or disaster lies ahead. And the same emotions keep resurfacing time and again until we listen and say 'okay, I'm ready to face this.' And uncomfortable as this may be, we listen and take action to do something to change how we feel or the circumstances. When you are swept up in the emotional moment, know that you are capable of handling it. Your child's behaviour is not you, but you have within you all you need to dissolve the situation, just as you have within you the means to provoke the situation and make it worse than it really is. Simply put, you have the capability to either make things better or worse. Knowing this, we can no longer abstain from our responsibility to resolve matters in any given situation, even if our children have triggered us in some way. Whatever emotions our children evoke in us, that emotion was not present prior to the incident or unwanted behaviour, and it only continues to exist if we allow it. You are not your emotions and your emotions are not you. Given time and a few deep slow breathes in and out to focus your mind in the present, the unwanted emotion within you will soon pass. Your child, though, is governed by their emotions so they'll still be tantruming or misbehaving, but that's okay because now you can deal with it appropriately.

Same child, expressing the same unwanted behaviour, but being approached differently by the pacifier instead of antagonist, resulting in a different outcome, hopefully where everyone comes away feeling okay or even better than before the situation occurred.

We've already said, when we allow our children to make their own choices, they lack resistance (remember My Little Welsh Girl outfit story?) and the repercussions of stretching our children like rubber bands.

Whatever we resist or fight will persist. The power is not in fighting, it's in peace. Whatever situation you are in, whoever you are with, the peace you bring is what illuminates your power of presence.

BE INSPIRING

However, as we already know, the influential role model is never perfect, and no one can expect us parents to be perfect either. But we can always try to be a better role model to our children today than the one we were yesterday, and we can be even better tomorrow than we are today. That way, we can serve as an inspiration to our children.

A little self-reflection can help us to consciously notice our influence and improve on areas we feel we are not making a positive impression. By being the best role models that we possibly can be, we inspire our children to be the best that they can be.

Our children are going to copy us, and we can't change that!

We are their models, and they are simply modelling our behaviours.

Once we know or understand something, it's impossible to unknow it, then we have a responsibility as we are no longer ignorant to the truth. We can no longer hide behind not knowing. We've become smarter when we've learnt something new, so we have to be proactive as we know that what we do or don't do does make a huge difference. Now, we can and do have a duty to teach our children, there's no more excuses, having the knowledge means we just need the time and inclination to do so.

The only thing that we can do is do our best to be someone worth copying, and someone who our children can be proud of. We all remember those bringers of peace; they did have a power of presence that lit up the world.

Jesus, Gandhi, Mother Teresa, and Nelson Mandela all had a tough time influencing and inspiring others in the beginning, but look how many billions of people they did and still do inspire in the world today.

They make being an inspiring parent and role model look easy!

Positively influencing our children when they are young will make the world a better place for everyone.

If they notice us being loving, kind, inspirational, appreciative, and empathetic, then this is who they will become.

As parents, we contribute greatly toward our children's aspirations and self-esteem, and how we pursue our own ambitions will impact theirs.

We have to lead by example by living the life we want to live and being the person we want our children to become. Especially if we want them to follow their dreams and succeed in life.

In the words of Gandhi, you have to 'be the change that you wish to see...'

As parents, we have the great privilege, power, and ability to create happy, healthy, and successful children.

We don't need a lot of money, a good job, or an education to give them these gifts.

All you need is to be able to give them the best possible you that you can give.

And you do have the power to do that. You are now a powerful parent; all the power is in your hands.

Your child needs nothing or no one other than you.

FINAL WORD

I MAGINE, NOW—EVERY DAY as a joyful happy time with your child, full of love and laughter and learning opportunities. A time you can cherish both now in the present and also as a fond memory in the future. The truth is, we can enjoy picnics in the park and building sandcastles on the beach with our little ones when we understand there's no other family more unique and perfect as our own. Feel free now to let go of the old illusions that everyone else is having an easier more fun time at parenting, let go of the control, go with the flow, and for once, enjoy the moment, even at the most mundane of times such as taking your child to the dentist. Every single minute of your day is your life, enjoy today, tomorrow never comes.

Of course, there will still be times when disputes happen, and your child will behave in inappropriate ways that upset you, but now you can easily deal with those times and that behaviour, whatever it might be. You can reinforce this by picturing the scene, your worst-case scenario, and see yourself managing it in a calm, relaxed manner, feel how good that feels as you listen to the confident, yet loving way you are speaking to your child. Practice this a few times in your mind before you go to sleep at night or when you wake in the morning, this will prepare you in advance, building your self confidence in your parenting abilities.

No shock to discover then that 'You' are the catalyst for desirable behaviour, and you may or may not be surprised to know that you have the resources within you to manage unwanted behaviour. There's no outside influence or authority or help that can do better than you yourself. Trust in yourself, tap into that inner strength, courage, and confidence, and unleash the power that you possess. That power is positive, don't be afraid to own it, your strength will be your power. It's always been there and always will be, but you have to summon it. Despite its ever-presence, by the time parents come to me for help with managing their children's behaviour, they are usually at the end of their tether. They've read every book or blog and spoken to everybody about the problem. Their focus has been on the external problem itself, not on the solution within, and that's caused a lot of confusion. It's easy to get lost in the sea of information out there, you have to be careful not to get bogged down or sink in despair.

It's good to remember that unwanted or difficult behaviour didn't develop overnight, and it won't disappear that quickly either. So, go easy on yourself as well as your child, as it takes patience to change.

Change is possible though. And can be quicker than expected, I have worked as a Hypnotherapist with many clients who have had phobias or habits for thirty odd years that have changed within thirty minutes. Nothing is impossible.

However, these are adults who want to change because they understand how staying stuck is affecting them or those they love. Children, I have found, are not so clear cut.

Although they haven't had issues as long, and they are very open and receptive to change with their innocent, suggestable, impressionable, young minds, we have to understand, they are not the ones who think they have a problem or who have decided to change. It's usually a parent wants to change them.

Both parents and children develop habits over time, and are used to acting and reacting in a certain way, that's why I always suggest parents change themselves first.

The maxim I live by is:

'Nothing changes unless I do' or should that be 'Nothing changes unless you do?'

But don't try and do it all yourself. Get a team of family, friends, and teachers or other health care professionals involved in helping you out. They will tend to know and better understand your unique, individual child rather than generalised information taken from books or the internet.

This book was written with love for parents and children in a generalised, broad term. Meaning, I have not taken into account any additional needs or children with disabilities. This book's central focus has been upon changing the parent's perceptions on behaviour, rather than changing the child. However, if you believe your child has a disability affecting their behaviour such as Asperger's, Autism, or ADD, or ADHD, then you will need to seek further help from a professional who can support you and your child appropriately. Meltdowns and tantrums are not the same, and the triggers are different also.

Help is out there, and there's no shame, embarrassment, or stigma attached to either needing or wanting help, so reach out for support. At least then you can parent your child more positively and effectively when you can understand their behaviour.

Most importantly, don't worry.

Remember: 'There's no war where love is concerned, and when love is the central motivation.' All that matters, when it comes to your child and parenting, is that you enjoy each other's company. To do this, you need to stay present and conscious in the moments you share together.

Having read this far, you can safely say that you are obviously a very loving parent. Not perfect, because there simply is no perfect parent and there is no perfect child, they do not exist. But what you hopefully now realise is that you are the perfect parent for your child.

And that your child is perfectly them, temper tantrums and all!

No one else could ever take the place of you or your child. Even a second, third, or fourth child will have their own unique place in your heart that cannot be replaced or replicated by another. Either way, your child is the present so enjoy and appreciate every moment you share.

However they arrived in your life—planned for, unexpected, adopted, or fostered, they are all individuals in their own right, perfect in every way, with limitless capabilities and infinite possibilities ahead of them. Ready and waiting for you to unwrap their layers and discover who they are and who they can become with your love and support.

Each one, like a single snowflake, is unique, but they're behaviour is not so unique. I want to tell you, as your children get older, parenting gets easier. But I won't lie, now as a mum to two teenagers, it's a shock!

You go from telling them what to do, to them telling you what to do. Dressing them, to them giving you style and fashion advice. Finally, I understand what my parents meant by 'I talk too fast in a language that doesn't exist. I'm unjustly embarrassed by those who gave me life and fund everything, and I'm constantly on the defensive like the world is against me.'

It only took me forty-two years and my own teenagers to teach me the error of my ways, but the best lessons always come to those who wait.

Karma's a promise from a God who looks on and laughs at all us parents at some time.

I can honestly say from experience though, that learning to understand our children while young and talking and listening to them works.

Hormones and peer pressure will affect them as they get older, but if the channel of communication is open and honest, they will turn to you for advice, and they will listen. Sometimes, conversations can be awkward, but if you find they are talking to you about awkward stuff, that's a good sign.

I have never hit my children or tried to intentionally make them feel bad, but they have always listened and understood what I have said to them and taken onboard advice.

I treat them with the respect they deserve, and as a result, they respect me.

As teens, they still go to bed when we tell them to, they still surrender their electronic devices by nine pm (although this is currently under review), and they are still happy, healthy, and successful. And they love us as parents.

Yes, there will always be a new stage and phase around the corner. As soon as you join the world of parenting, that's guaranteed. But as powerful, influential role models, hopefully, we now feel empowered in our roles rather than powerless.

I hope this book has helped you in some way, if so, I would love to hear all about it either by leaving me a book review on Amazon or via social media. If you would like to email me personally with an issue, you can email me at emma@happychildcare.club. I may not always be able to answer every question personally, but I endeavour to cover them in blog posts or future books.

And if you need any help with implementing routines and haven't already read my other book in this series, *The Confident Parent's Guide to Raising a Happy, Healthy & Successful Child*. I recommend you read that book next to increase confidence in your proactive parenting, available from Amazon and all good book stockists now.

You can also tag or make contact with me through my social media platforms using the following hashtags:

#ConfidentParents
#PowerfulParents
#PresentParenting
#ProactiveParenting
#ProactiveParents

My social media are as follows:

https://twitter.com/EmmaGrantAuthor
https://www.facebook.com/1977therapy
https://emmagrantauthor.com/
https://www.instagram.com/emgrantauthor
https://www.happychildcare.club
https://www.facebook.com/pg/EmmandPaulGrant
https://www.instagram.com/happychildcarepentwyn

Finally, I will finish with a poem I wrote for school when I was twelve years of age.

I don't know if it was a reflection of how I felt as a child, but it seems fitting to include it here in this book. Thankfully, I did take my own advice, and although I did not view it as a mistake, I did think of those sperms and their generation, hence my own children and this book.

ONE LITTLE SPERM

Brought to this earth by no choice of mine,
Just one little sperm in a short space of time.
That one night no one knew of me,
Nine months later I was for all to see.
Nothing to be proud of I know that now,
But at that time, I was gold somehow?
Unprepared for the trials of life,
That future that was to carry all my strife.
So, before I make their mistake again,
I'll think of the sperm for the generation of men!

—*Emma Brand [Grant] [age 12]*

So, be nice to your little ones now, for it won't be long before they are dressing you and doling out fashion advice. Teaching you how to interpret their slang language while translating reality shows for you (Yes, we do need subtitles) dominated by grownups young enough to be your own kids!

Enjoy your kids while they're young and be kind to them always. They really will choose your destiny when they are older. For now, all us long suffering, reflective parents can do at this time is bite our tongue and let our children think they are right.

One day, like us as parents, they'll be sorry for the error of their ways and thank us for our love.

Stay Powerful, Stay Proactive, and, most importantly, Stay Present!

Your child is the Present, enjoy the Gift!

Love Em x

GLOSSARY OF TERMS

You may come across some or all of these terms in my series of books. In case you aren't familiar with my books, below is a glossary of the most common phrases or words and what they mean.

Auto Pilot Parents or Parenting: means a parent who is distracted or who responds, reacts, and behaves in a habitual way,] without thinking about what they are doing or why.

Perfect: perfect in the eyes and expectations of others.

Powerful Parents or Power: refers to parents who have influence and can use this influence to positively teach, guide, and coach.

Present Parenting: being Present means being conscious in the moment.

Proactive Parents or Proactive Parenting or a Proactive Approach: the word 'proactive' here means taking action in advance or being involved. It means pre-empting and preventing issues before they occur. Prevention is better than a cure!

The U URSELF Routine: a mnemonic for You Yourself, and stands for a routine that consists of the following:

> U Time
> Us Time
> Recreation
> Sleep
> Esteem
> Love
> Food

DISCLAIMER

This is a non-fiction book, therefore, the anecdotes within the book are all true. If they were made up stories, they would be a work of fiction, not facts. However, no individuals have been named except on the one occasion when referring to a past teacher of mine, in this case, this was a made-up name to protect the identity of that person. The sole intention of this book is help us to learn from past parenting /childcare professionals and their experiences so we can make positive changes. It is not intended in any way to judge or condemn anyone or the experiences they have encountered or created. All the opinions and beliefs expressed throughout are my own.

Over the years, parents and children have come and gone to and from my setting, yet all the situations and parenting issues remain the same. Therefore, if you can identify with a story it's probably not you, but if you're like most of us parents, there's a chance it could be too!

All information is based on my own personal opinions and experiences from my role as a Mum, Registered Childminder, Parent Coach, and Hypnotherapist. Although based on real life scenarios and facts, I do not claim to heal, diagnose, or treat anyone. All concerns regarding your child, whether physical, psychological or emotional should be addressed by a qualified professional, such as your own GP. I offer recommendations to help you as a parent to manage and enjoy the parenting journey based on what I have found has worked over the years with other parents, but I do not claim my way to be the best for everyone or the only way. Take from this book what feels right, what suits, and what works best for you and your child and family and follow your own parental intuition and instincts always.

ACKNOWLEDGEMENTS

Thank you to all the many parents and children I have had the pleasure and privilege to look after and work with over the past sixteen years at Happy Childcare. Without you all, this book would never have been written, so thank you all very much.

Also, special thanks to Hayley Paige, my publisher, and the team at Notebook Publishing (Marni, my editor; and Mark, my cover designer): your support and creativity has been invaluable.

I would also like to acknowledge a higher power of love's influence— through my words I was guided, thank you.

ABOUT THE AUTHOR

Emma Grant is the author of *The Confident Parent's Guide to Raising a Happy, Healthy & Successful Child*, a Mum, Hypnotherapist, Nutritional Therapist, and Parenting Coach/Counsellor.

She has also been a Registered Childminder for the past sixteen years with a Level 5 Diploma in Leadership and Management in Children's Care, Learning, and Development.

She works alongside her husband, living in Cardiff UK with their teenage children.

www.ingramcontent.com/pod-product-compliance
Lightning Source LLC
Chambersburg PA
CBHW072342090426
42741CB00012B/2891